Lionel Messi

A Biography of the Argentine Superstar

(The Secrets and Skills of the Best Player in the World)

Jose Montgomery

Published By **Bengion Cosalas**

Jose Montgomery

All Rights Reserved

Lionel Messi: A Biography of the Argentine Superstar (The Secrets and Skills of the Best Player in the World)

ISBN 978-1-7782825-6-0

No part of this guidebook shall be reproduced in any form without permission in writing from the publisher except in the case of brief quotations embodied in critical articles or reviews.

Legal & Disclaimer

The information contained in this book is not designed to replace or take the place of any form of medicine or professional medical advice. The information in this book has been provided for educational & entertainment purposes only.

The information contained in this book has been compiled from sources deemed reliable, and it is accurate to the best of the Author's knowledge; however, the Author cannot guarantee its accuracy and validity and cannot be held liable for any errors or omissions. Changes are periodically made to this book. You must consult your doctor or get professional medical advice before using any of the suggested remedies, techniques, or information in this book.

Upon using the information contained in this book, you agree to hold harmless the Author from and against any damages, costs, and expenses, including any legal fees potentially resulting from the application of any of the information provided by this guide. This disclaimer applies to any damages or injury caused by the use and application, whether directly or indirectly, of any advice or information presented, whether for breach of contract, tort, negligence, personal injury, criminal intent, or under any other cause of action.

You agree to accept all risks of using the information presented inside this book. You need to consult a professional medical practitioner in order to ensure you are both able and healthy enough to participate in this program.

Table Of Contents

Chapter 1: The Boy Of Rosario 1

Chapter 2: Beginning Years Of Lionel Messi 6

Chapter 3: Experiencing The Talents 17

Chapter 4: Lionel's Adventure Through.. 23

Chapter 5: Spark Of A Legend 28

Chapter 6: The Rivalries And Triumphs .. 34

Chapter 7: Unleashing Messi's Record-Breaking Brilliance 40

Chapter 8: The Tragic Weight Of Being Great... 45

Chapter 9: The Messi-Ronaldo Rivalry ... 55

Chapter 10: Messi's Humanitarian Work And Personal Life 61

Chapter 11: Lionel's Move To Paris Saint-Germain 67

Chapter 12: Messi's Legacy The Retirement Options After 2023............. 73

Chapter 13: Early Life 79

Chapter 14: Joining Fc Barcelona Academy 90

Chapter 15: Record-Breaking Seasons . 103

Chapter 16: The Overall Impact 113

Chapter 17: Life Lessons Taught From Lionel Messi 128

Chapter 18: Humanitarian Work It Is The Leo Messi Foundation 137

Chapter 19: Affairs And Football Balancing 149

Chapter 20: Club Career 162

Chapter 1: The Boy Of Rosario

In the past, in the bustling town in Rosario, Argentina, there was a boy who was named Lionel Messi. At an early age it was evident that Lionel was a gifted player in the sport of football. Born on the 24th June 1987, into a poor family Lionel was raised in a community in which football was more than an athletic event It was an integral part to live.

From the first moment Lionel began walking and walk, he would be seen running his worn-out ball around the streets that were narrow in Rosario as he dodged obstacles, imagine himself as a superhero playing on the biggest stage. His passion for soccer is infectious and he spread excitement and happiness to relatives and friends. However, it was his unique aptitude and skill to stand out from all the others.

Even at his young age the extraordinary abilities of Lionel attracted the attention of his family members, who recognized his talents as well and urged him to follow his goals. The father of Lionel, Jorge, recognized the talents of his son and he became his greatest fan. Together, they'd spend endless hours training, perfecting the skills of Lionel, while fantasizing about the future of football.

Over the course of time the Lionel's skills was able to grow. He was a part of the local soccer club Grandoli in which he amazed his coaches, teammates as well as opponents with his amazing speed incredible dribbling skills, captivating dribbling technique, and precise passes. The results he scored on the pitch was not unnoticed and soon scouts of the elite football academy Newell's Old Boys, came to his house.

The family of Lionel, while reluctant to let their child star away, realized that it was an excellent chance. They knew that in order to develop Lionel's abilities and let him to realize his maximum potential, sacrifices must be to be made. Through a tearful heart and a tearful goodbye, they said farewell to their son who was dearly loved, seeing him set off on an adventure that would define his future.

In Newell's Old Boys, Lionel was faced with new challenges and fierce opposition. However, his determination, coupled with his dazzling talent, shined through. He soon rose through the ranks of football, enthralling supporters and leaving an arc of amazed fans following his footsteps. The football world started to take note of the upcoming Argentine star.

When Lionel's fame grew, as did the expectations of the people who watched his dazzling displays of talent and skill. Rosario was a city captivated by the enchantment of their local idol. The child from the streets was now an inspiring figure who represented potential and hope for the generation that was aspiring to success.

The path to success was not without it's own set of difficulties. When Lionel's popularity rose however, he was confronted with a daunting problem: a deficiency in growth hormone that could have a negative impact on his hopes. The disease required costly medical treatments that Lionel's family was unable to pay for. The appearance of the journey would come to an end before the journey had began.

Then, destiny came through in the form of FC Barcelona, one of the world's most famous soccer teams. They saw Lionel's incredible ability and potential. the sporting director at FC Barcelona, Carles Rexach, was extremely impressed with his abilities that he gave an agreement in the form of a napkin. A simple act of trust was not just a turning point in Lionel's career but also ignited a fire which would change forever the direction of football's history.

Amid a deep sadness, Lionel bid farewell to his dear friend Rosario and began an exciting new journey in Barcelona. This was an incredibly difficult decision as a teen who had left everything he was familiar with and loving to follow his dream abroad. However, Lionel was determined not to shun challenges. Instead, he took advantage of the chance with a relentless determination and a constant thirst for achievement.

It was not known the arrival of Lionel Messi in Barcelona was to usher in an unparalleled era and redefine what it means to be the top footballer on the planet. However, that's a tale to be told in a different chapter, a story of determination, triumph and a unbreakable determination that drove Lionel Messi to unimaginable heights and permanently etch his name into the history of the greatest footballers.

Chapter 2: Beginning Years Of Lionel Messi

Within the field of football, very few players resonate with the same intensity like Lionel Messi. He is renowned for his extraordinary ability, extraordinary skills and unmatched successes, Messi has solidified his status as one of football's best footballers of the past. Every legend has its humble beginnings and the tale of his early days is nothing short of captivating. From his early years at Rosario, Argentina, to his meteoric rise to Barcelona Messi's story is an example of his perseverance as well as his tenacity and capabilities. In this essay we explore the early years of Lionel Messi, exploring his beginnings, struggles early on, and pivotal events that helped shape him into the footballer he is currently.

I. A Star was Born 24 June 1987

A summer day in the sun on a sunny day in Rosario, Argentina, Celia and Jorge Messi welcomed their third child, Lionel Andres

Messi, to the world. Since the age of a child, Messi displayed an innate love for football and was fascinated by the game as the moth that catches a fire. As a child, he lived in the humble community that was La Bajada, he spent many hours throwing a ball on the streets and dazzling people with his innate skill.

II. Insufficient Growth Hormone as well as the ability to overcome adversity

Although Messi's ability in the field was evident but his path to success wasn't without challenges. In the age of eleven the soccer player was diagnosed with a hormone called growth insufficiency. The condition could have slowed his hopes that he would become an elite soccer player. The price of treatment that involved daily injections was out of reach for Messi's family. But, fate intervened and Messi was noticed by Carles Rexach who was the sports director for FC Barcelona, during a game in Spain. In recognition of Messi's incredible potential, Rexach gave him an agreement on napkins and assured that the young Argentine received the required medical attention and an opportunity to fulfill his goals.

III. The relocation to Barcelona as well as The La Masia Experience

At 13 years of age, Messi and his family moved to Barcelona which is where he was accepted into the highly regarded FC Barcelona youth academy, La Masia. As he adjusted to a brand new culture and a new language and a completely new culture, Messi faced numerous challenges. Yet, his determination and his innate ability, allowed him to endure. With the help of legendary coaches, and supported by highly skilled players, Messi honed his abilities improving his skills as well as his tactical knowledge of football.

IV. The Rise of the Top From the Youth Team to the First Team First Team

As Messi moved up the ranks of Barcelona His talent was more and more difficult to overlook. In 2004 Messi made his debut in Barcelona's Barcelona B team, awe-inspiring players and coaches alike by his speedy pace as well as his dazzling dribbling skills and his ruthless finishing. The following year, in October 2005 at age 18 years old, Messi made his debut for the team under the direction of coach Frank Rijkaard, marking the start of an incredible adventure that would change the game of football.

V. Overcoming Setbacks: Injury and the road to Redemption

Despite the early success, Messi faced a series of setbacks, in the form of injuries that recurred which threatened to halt his professional career. Muscle issues hampered his progress and injuries, he was forced to spend months in the hospital, going through exhausting rehabilitation procedures. But Messi's strength and determination never wavered as he bounced into action stronger every time. With the help of the medical team at Barcelona as well as his indomitable work ethic Messi was back on the soccer field with a accomplishment that surpassed the heights he had previously achieved.

VI. International Stardom International Stardom: This is the Argentine National Team

Although Messi was a star in Barcelona but his time in his Argentine national team was tougher. Even with his extraordinary potential, many critics have doubted his dedication to the national team. Yet, Messi's determination to excel at the highest level let up. Messi was the one to lead Argentina to victory at 2005's U-20 FIFA World Cup, impressing the crowds with his mesmerizing display. Through the years his commitment and determination led Argentina to many major finals including this year's FIFA World Cup and the Copa America, where he had his first taste of glory in 2021.

Lionel Messi's rise from being a child of Rosario and on to become a worldwide soccer legend is testament to his unrelenting determination, perseverance, and exceptional talent. Through overcoming numerous challenges, such as medical issues and personal setbacks His unflinching dedication and innate skill have set himself apart from other players. Beginning in La Masia to lifting numerous trophy in the ranks of FC Barcelona and the Argentine national team Messi always pushed the limits of what's possible in a football court. His experiences serve as an example toChapter 13 of Messi's legacy and retirement Options in 2023.

A Story of Immortality and the Farewell

The year is 2023 in which Lionel Messi stands at the crossing point of his iconic career. The Argentine master has dazzled footballers from all over the world for more than two decades creating a lasting impression on the game. His talents keep awestruck, questions remain about the direction of his career as well as his eventual retirement decision.

Messi's Legacy:

For a full understanding of the magnitude of Messi's legacy, you must reflect on his impact on the game of football. Beginning at Barcelona in which he climbed up the ranks in La Masia, to the many trophies, records and personal awards he accumulated his greatness, Messi's brilliance has always been an enduring presence across the soccer landscape.

His incredible dribbling abilities sharp vision and his slick finishing skills has made him a difficult opponent for defenses, and an absolute delight for the fans. Messi's record-breaking goals have changed things that were once believed to be to be possible. His partnership with Barcelona resulted in a period of dominance that will be remembered in the history of football.

His legacy isn't just on the playing field. His humbleness, sporting spirit as well as unwavering commitment to his sport has made him a inspiration for players from all over the world. His charitable efforts, which are facilitated by his foundation, the Leo Messi Foundation and collaborations with organisations like UNICEF has benefited many children's lives and affirmed his place as a world-renowned ambassador of soccer.

Retirement Questions:

In the moment that Messi enters the final stages of his playing career, the decision to quit becomes the subject of discussion and debate. The abrasions and wear of professional football and the physical demands of elite games, have raised questions regarding whether he'll be able to remain at the top of the game.

On the other hand Messi's unbeatable skill and soccer-related intelligence suggests that he can defy the age and perform in the top leagues throughout the years. His capacity to change his style of play, cope with the physical changes with age and help aid in the development of his squad is a clear indication that retiring is not a far possibility.

The toll of a lengthy and successful life cannot be ignored. The physical strain, the stress of being constantly scrutinized, and the burden that comes with carrying the hopes of the nation could cause a lot of stress to even the strongest athletes. When Messi is contemplating retirement, thoughts about his health and well-being in the long run as well as his family's life and the wish to begin a new phase outside of the game could come in.

The End of the Line:

If the day comes when Messi to leave the sport that defined his entire life and shaped his career, it's bound to be a time of tremendous importance. All football fans are expected in a moment of celebration for one of the most successful players who have ever graced the field, and feelings will be intense when teammates, fans, as well as rivals, say goodbye to a legend.

The moment that Messi retires, whatever it comes the case, will be accompanied with a feeling of loss to the game. His departure will leave an unfilled void that can't be quickly filled. It will also serve as a time of reflection when the soccer community will celebrate numerous memories, excellence, and the motivation Messi has given throughout his entire career.

After his retirement, Messi will have the chance to build his legacy through new methods. Be it by coaching youngsters, or following different interests, his influence in the sport will never cease to resonate. In addition, his contributions off the field to philanthropy, as well as a social advocate concerns, will be an affirmation of his character and values that he cherishes.

In the midst of Lionel Messi navigates the final seasons of his legendary career, his name is shining brightly. His unrivaled accomplishments on the field, as well as his affable manner and charitable endeavors Messi established a benchmark of quality that will be a part of the fabric throughout the generations. Making the decision to retire at any time to pass, is a highly personal decision, taking into account the importance of health, family as well as personal satisfaction.

If it is time for Messi to leave all football fans will gather to honor his remarkable contribution to the game. Although his loss will be felt but his influence will continue for the next generation of players, and giving us a reminder of the incredible results which can be created with dedication, skill as well as a constant love of the game.

Chapter 3: Experiencing The Talents

The sun was beginning to set, as youthful Lionel Messi kicked a worn-out soccer ball into the wall of his tiny community located in Rosario, Argentina. The streets of Rosario were buzzing with laughter and occasional shouts of excitement from children playing soccer on every surface. Of all the children, Lionel was a standout in a way that was not just due to his petite stature, but due to his amazing aptitude and love to play the sport.

Six years ago, at the age of the age of six Messi began playing for the club's local young team Grandoli. The father of the team, Jorge acknowledged his Son's exceptional capabilities and determined to help him achieve his dream of being an elite soccer player. Lionel's talents were evident right at the beginning. His speed, agility and instinctual sensitivity to the game have left his opponents confused and his fellow players stunned.

Messi's abilities quickly spread and caught the notice of scouts from famous Newell's Old Boys, one of Argentina's most prestigious youth academy. They were eager to observe the young star in person. They were able to watch as Messi effortlessly dribbled past the opponents, seamlessly weaved through small spaces, then unleashed devastating shots that were precise. Scouts realized they'd come across something extraordinary.

Besotted by his amazing abilities, Newell's Old Boys offered Messi an opportunity to join their academy. It was a dream coming real for the young star as well as his family. Lionel took the chance and fought for it, dedicating himself to training and developing his talents naturally. He worked for hours on shooting, dribbling and ball control. He was always striving to get better.

With the help of seasoned coaches, Messi's talents grew more. He was able to absorb every single piece of advice and honed his techniques and understanding about the sport. He was a tireless worker and determination distinguished him from the rest of his teammates. Each training session was approached with an unending desire to growth, and never satisfied with an average performance.

The more Messi's talents developed and his fame grew, so did his skills. His performance at youth events made fans and teams astonished. The coaches of professional clubs from across Argentina started to pay attention. The prodigy's young age gave him an uncanny ability to create scoring opportunities and squeezing through barriers as if he were ghosts. His field vision was unmatched and he seemed be a natural at understanding the game.

A few days ago, as a team was competing at a regional event the scout of Barcelona one of the most famous teams in the world found himself on the sidelines. The scout had heard stories about a promising Argentine player, but witnessing Messi perform live was a completely different experience. The scout was aware that he'd discovered a gem hidden in the dirt.

In awe of Messi's talents The Barcelona soccer scout was on the move in no time. He contacted the family of Lionel and told them about the club's desire in signing the soccer star's young talent. The deal was enticing, and Lionel as well as his family took the pivotal decision to move to Spain to leave behind their home and surroundings, beginning a new journey.

At thirteen, Messi began his journey at La Masia, Barcelona's renowned youth academy. Messi quickly adjusted to the new environment, looking to establish himself as one of the most talented young players across the globe. Even though he initially struggled in overcoming homesickness as well as the difficulties of adjusting to a completely new style of living and a new culture his determination was never slowed.

With the help of skilled coaches, Messi's talents kept growing. The player he trained with were later to become his friends and teammates such as Xavi Hernandez, and Andres Iniesta. Together, they laid the basis of what is now called one of the most successful soccer teams ever created.

Messi's path from a tinier community in Rosario towards the grand stadium at Camp Nou was filled with challenges, however his exceptional ability and dedication to his sport made him a pillar of great success. His distinctive approach to football, highlighted by his dazzling dribbling abilities as well as lightning-fast speed and incredible goal scoring ability, has captivated soccer fans across the globe.

At some point, Lionel Messi would go through the ranks to smash numerous records and win a variety of titles and be awarded numerous accolades such as Six Ballon d'Or awards. The player would be a legend as a symbol for excellence within the field of soccer.

However, it all began as a child living in Rosario who was kicking his worn out soccer ball on the walls of his home, recognizing his skills and never turning for a second.

So, the third chapter of Lionel Messi's incredible journey ended which set the stage to the upcoming chapter full of triumphs, struggles and a quest for excellence.

Chapter 4: Lionel's Adventure Through

In the sprawling city of Barcelona one day, a youth known as Lionel Messi entered the hallowed fields of FC Barcelona's youth school, La Masia, unaware that he would soon start a journey which will alter the direction of soccer history.

Messi showed an incredible ability to play the game at a very young time. When he was just 13he took his life-changing decision to relocate to Spain to leave his home and all that he had known, in order to follow his ambitions.

When he arrived to La Masia, Messi found himself within a crowded environment that was brimming with young talent. Despite his petite physical stature and calm manner, Messi had an uncommon and natural ability to control the ball with incredible ability to control the ball with precision. His coaches soon noticed his remarkable skills and in no time Messi was the glittering bright star of the school.

Inside the confines in La Masia, Messi honed his skills tirelessly. He worked for hours on practicing his dribbling, passing and shooting technique with an endless desire to get better. The dedication to his work and commitment could not be matched even at this young age. The coaches and players were amazed by his uncanny ability to understand the game as well as his speedy agility. He left the opposition stunned and fans amazed.

As Messi made his way through the ranks, it was obvious that he was bound to excel. He swiftly transitioned from Barcelona's young team into Barcelona B, the club's reserve squad, and kept impressing fans with his impressive performance. While playing for Barcelona B that he caught the attention of first-team director, Frank Rijkaard, who gave him his first senior appearance during a friendly game in a friendly match against FC Porto.

The world was set to see the creation of a supernova. On the 1st of May, the year 2005

Messi played his debut for Barcelona's Barcelona first team. He became the first player in history to take on the famed Blaugrana jersey for the official game. His impact was immediately felt, when Messi scored his first goal for the club only a few weeks following. Both the press and fans was captivated by his natural ability and his maturity that was beyond age.

From then on Messi's fame rose. His actions on the field were simply amazing and earned him the name "The Flea" for his mysterious movements and lightning-quick speed. He had the ability to alter the course of play on his own with his speed, causing opponents to fall behind when he swung through defences like a bolt lightning.

The remarkable career of Messi in the club of FC Barcelona was marked by an incredible number of accomplishments and records. He broke the club's record-breaking score record for scoring, beating the legend Cesar Rodriguez. He was the first footballer in the history of football who scored 91 goals within the course of a calendar year. Each year, he took home the highly sought-after FIFA Ballon d'Or award, making him the most successful athlete of his generation.

Lionel Messi's stint in FC Barcelona's academy for youth has not just helped him develop into an outstanding footballer, but it taught him the principles of endurance dedication, humility, and respect. In his long time at FC Barcelona, he was fiercely loyal to the team that gave him everything and became the epitomization of Barcelona's "Mes qu'est-ce que tu club" principle.

When Messi's stint in FC Barcelona ultimately came to the end of his career, his name remains forever in the pages of history in football. His amazing skills, unmatchable successes, and unwavering devotion has made him a sports icon. In the years to come, he will continue his quest to the outskirts of Catalonia the mark he has left on this beautiful sport can serve as a beacon of hope to soccer players in the next generation around the globe, and reminds the youngsters that their dreams can be fulfilled through perseverance determination, dedication, and an confidence that is never shaken.

Lionel Messi's incredible development from a young talent at FC Barcelona's youth academy, to becoming a global soccer legend is testimony to his extraordinary ability, determination, and the hospitable environment created through La Masia. This is the story of triumph against adversity of a child who believed in his dreams and who surpassed his expectations. His success did not just elevate him to the highest level of soccer, but it also consolidated FC Barcelona's standing as a proving ground for excellence. His experience in La Masia will always be recognized as the starting point of a remarkable journey that forever changed the face of football.

Chapter 5: Spark Of A Legend

The passion for sports that Lionel had was fostered by his loving family and especially his grandma, Celia.

Celia recognized her grandson's potential, urged Lionel to follow his dream. She often accompanied him during matches and cheer at him from the sidelines. Although he was small the talents of Messi captivated all who observed him playing. His extraordinary abilities caught the eye of the scouts at FC Barcelona.

At the age of 13years old, Lionel Messi made a life-changing decision to quit his home and make the move towards Barcelona, Spain. It wasn't simple, since it was a decision to leave his home and family, as well as everything that he knew. The prospect being a part of one of the most famous football clubs brought him joy and determination.

Messi's first time during his time at La Masia, Barcelona's youth academy, proved to be a challenge. The separation from his parents and battling the barrier of language caused a lot of stress for the young star. Yet, his skill in the field was louder than any other language. And quickly, he was enjoying his new surroundings.

While Messi moved through Barcelona's young levels, his abilities were constantly evolving. His incredible acceleration, speed and control of the ball captivated the coaches and fans alike. At 16 Messi made his debut in the first team with Barcelona in a friendly game with FC Porto.

It didn't take too long for Messi to become a major player during competitive games. In 2004, he was the youngest player ever to achieve a goal in a match for Barcelona during a match in the league. This goal is a testimony to his unwavering determination and talent. Every time he played, Messi's confidence increased and he was able to become one of the key players in the squad.

The season 2005-2006 saw Barcelona participated in the highly coveted UEFA

Champions League. The promising young Messi played an integral role during their run to reach the finals. Through his fast and lightning-fast running along with his dazzling dribbles precise finishing, he was the enemy's worst nightmare.

In the final match against Arsenal and with the score being 1-1 Messi took advantage of the situation. Through a flurry in speed, Messi flew through a number of Arsenal players, before securing the ball into the goal. The goal was not just a way to secure the victory of Barcelona, but also signified Messi's debut on the biggest arena of European soccer.

The more famed Messi became and his ambitions grew, so did his thirst for the next level. The 2008-2009 campaign was the turning point of his career. He was a formidable attack trio that included Samuel Eto'o and Thierry Henry Together, they caused chaos on opposing defenses.

In that season, Messi's goal scoring ability soared to new levels. He scored 38 goals during La Liga, surpassing the previous record of real Madrid's Telmo Zarra in the year 1951. In addition, his performance led to him winning his FIFA World Player of the Year award. This established him as among the top athletes in the world.

The following seasons Messi's professional career continued to grow. Every season, he defied records easily, leaving people and experts stunned by his skills. The season of 2011-2012 was impressive, since Messi broke Gerd Muller's previous record for the highest number of goals scored in the calendar year.

The Argentine master's constant determination to be the best led Barcelona into numerous national and international victories. The teamwork of his teammates like Xavi Hernandez, and Andres Iniesta produced a captivating style of football that is known as "tiki-taka," which became the symbol of Barcelona's success.

The individual awards of Messi have accumulated and he was awarded his Ballon d'Or (FIFA World Player of the Year) award numerous times. His remarkable performances helped lead Barcelona to numerous national and international awards, including several La Liga titles and UEFA Champions League wins.

Lionel Messi's transformation from being a child from Rosario to becoming an international soccer icon is testimony to his dedication unfaltering and unparalleled ability. He changed the game by introducing a unique approach to play and has become an inspiration for future footballers around the world.

The success of Messi on the pitch was also a source of inspiration for countless youngsters in Argentina to follow their goals relentlessly. His humble beginnings and his climb to fame showed the world that, with perseverance and perseverance everything is achievable.

While Messi's football career is advancing and his influence in the field of football continues to be immense. Messi has been an icon of determination as well as excellence and humbleness, leaving an imprint on football and carving his name in the top tier of players to ever have graced the magnificent game.

Chapter 6: The Rivalries And Triumphs

The sunsets in Rosario, Argentina, had seen the birth of an soccer legend. Lionel Messi, a prodigious talent, walked the field with grace and ease, drawing the attention of Barcelona Scouts even at an early age. They recognized his potential for excellence, and in the year 2003, aged of 16 Lionel Messi left his homeland to the bustling city that are Barcelona, Spain.

When he arrived at Barcelona the rivalry between Messi and Cristiano Ronaldo took form. They appeared set to clash in the biggest stage ever -- the FIFA World Cup. The two styles of each provoked passionate debates between fans across the world. Messi's vision, agility as well as dazzling dribbling abilities are masked by Ronaldo's strength as well as speed and thunderous attacks on goals.

The El-Classico Showdown

When Messi excelled at Barcelona and Madrid, he was the center of the club, and led to numerous national as well as European wins. The fierce competition among Barcelona as well as Real Madrid added another layer to the messi-Ronaldo saga. In the end, El Clasico clashes became eagerly looked forward to events that split soccer fans across the globe. There was speculation about which team would emerge the top of the pile, while Messi's delicate skill competed with Ronaldo's ferocious force.

It is the Battle for International Glory

Although Messi's successes in Barcelona was growing, his journey to glory on the international stage was not without difficulties. In Argentina the team, he was subject to numerous heartbreaking near-misses. In 2014, the FIFA World Cup Final saw an opportunity for Messi to establish his place among the top players ever. But the German Juggernaut won, leaving Messi feeling a bit disappointed and beset by the wrath of his critics.

A Golden Ball-related Controversy Begins

A particular issue that was a part of Messi was his battle to secure the famed FIFA World Cup with the Argentinian senior side. Despite his unparalleled athleticism on the field, the gold trophy was to be elusive. Many critics believed that he did not have an edge of power to lead his team to glory on the international stage and cast doubt on his claims to be the most outstanding player on earth.

Triumph at Last

But 2021 added an exciting twist to the plot. After spending 17 years in Barcelona, Messi decided to take on new challenges. He was signed to Paris Saint-Germain (PSG), which is where he formed an impressive alliance with superstars Kylian Mbappe as well as Neymar Jr. The group, nicknamed the "Golden Trident"" caused a flurry of excitement in football fans.

It's the Golden Ball controversy that has Revisited

Messi's switch to PSG brought back the discussion about and the Ballon d'Or. There were those who believed that his performances in the club of PSG and the Copa America triumph with Argentina and finally earned him recognition as one of the top players on the planet. Others argued that they believed that Ballon d'Or should be awarded in accordance with club performance and Robert Lewandowski's outstanding season with Bayern Munich making a compelling argument.

Battle for Recognition Battle for Recognition

In the year 2022, as the FIFA World Cup approached, Messi and Ronaldo faced yet another battle. Both were conscious that winning a World Cup victory would significantly improve their odds to win the Ballon d'Or. The world of football held its breath waiting to see the final battle between two generations of talent.

The Final Act

The World Cup unfolded with a sequence of thrilling games that showed the brilliance of Messi, Ronaldo, and others who are football legends. In the final match, Argentina faced France, and the setting was ready for the match between Messi and Ronaldo which had been a favorite for decades.

A Golden Ball-related Controversy Has Settled

The final whistle was blown, Messi and Argentina emerged triumphant. Messi had taken his country to the top of world-class success. The incredible displays of Messi during the tournament won his the Golden Ball, cementing his position as a legend in the sport.

Lionel Messi's story, which was rife with triumphs, rivalries and debates, had come to the apex. Messi's exploits on the pitch were awe-inspiring to all audiences and earned him the respect of peers, fans as well as pundits. There was the Ballon d'Or debate may have been a raging debate, but Messi's contribution to the game was greater than personal accolades. His singular blend of skill and determination created a lasting impression on the history of football, making him one of the top players that be a part of the game.

Chapter 7: Unleashing Messi's Record-Breaking Brilliance

It was the combination Pep Guardiola's tactical savvy and the extraordinary talents of Lionel Messi resulted in one of the most powerful periods in the history football. Under Guardiola's leadership in Barcelona between 2008 and 2012. Messi has achieved many records as well as achievements, establishing his position in the ranks of one of football's best players ever to grace the pitch. The chapter focuses on the remarkable collaboration with Guardiola with Messi and delve into the achievements and records Messi achieved under the direction of Guardiola. Catalan master.

The arrival Of Pep Guardiola:

Pep Guardiola became the manager at FC Barcelona in the summer of 2008 after an impressive stint with Barcelona B. Guardiola's appointment was a turning stage for the club because Guardiola took on the revolutionary tactic called "tiki-taka." The style of play that was based on possession concentrated on intricate passing high pressing and positional game, which allowed Messi to excel as a player in the attack system of the team.

The Perfect Mix:

The philosophy of Guardiola and Messi's distinctive ability proved an ideal match in footballing heaven. Guardiola was aware of Messi's extraordinary abilities and adapted the team's strategy in order to maximise his contribution. Utilizing Messi as the false nine in a position that let him roam free allowed him to create room for his teammates, and created Barcelona's attacks virtually impossible to stop.

Milestones and Records:

Score Record under Guardiola's direction, Messi shattered numerous scoring records. The 2011-2012 season was when he became the very first soccer player ever to record 50 goals during one league season beating the previous record, set by Gerd Muller. Messi is also the record holder for scoring the most goals within a calendar year. with a staggering of 91 goals during the year 2012.

Individual Awards: In the Guardiola period, Messi's achievements were rewarded with an incredible amount of prizes. He was awarded the FIFA Ballon d'Or award four consecutively between 2009 and 2012, establishing his position as the top athlete on earth. This feat of awe was never before seen during the history of the award.

Treble triumph: During the 2008-2009 football season, Barcelona, led by Guardiola and driven by Messi and Messi, earned an historic three-time treble. The club was crowned champions of La Liga, the Copa del Rey as well as the UEFA Champions League, completing an historic feat which demonstrated their power on both local as well as European arenas.

The perfect season under Guardiola's leadership during the 2010-2011 campaign, Barcelona produced what many believe was the best season. The club took home La Liga with a record-breaking 99 points and won the title in a staggering sixteen-point advantage over the second placed Real Madrid. In addition, this season witnessed Barcelona triumph in the UEFA Champions League, defeating Manchester United in the final at Wembley and with Messi taking the initiative.

Goal-scoring streaks: Messi's consistent scoring and the ability to get in the the net regularly were unmatched in the Guardiola period. Messi set a record in scoring consecutive league matches, hitting the net for 21 consecutive games in the season of 2012. The record beat the previous record that was set by Polish striker Teodor Pewterek.

Hat-Tricks: Messi's ability of scoring hat-tricks is another characteristic of his time with Guardiola. Through this period Messi scored a record 21 hat-tricks and further consolidated his standing as a prolific goal scorer. The hat-tricks were scored in a variety of tournaments like La Liga, the UEFA Champions League and the Copa del Rey.

The Pep Guardiola period at Barcelona saw Lionel Messi reach new heights setting records, and hitting records that seemed impossible. The tactical genius of Guardiola along with Messi's incredible talent made the perfect team that is forever remembered as the most exciting and thrilling soccer teams in history. Together, they were able to inspire generations of players and left an imprint on football, Messi writing his name into the records books through numerous achievements. His reign and Messi's record-breaking feats is forever cherished as an era of glory that will live in the history books of soccer.

Chapter 8: The Tragic Weight Of Being Great

Lionel Messi, widely regarded as one of the best footballers in history He has had a long and successful career full of successes and awards. Yet, one important tournament has always been elusive - his participation in the FIFA World Cup. In spite of his unquestionable ability and his success at club level, with FC Barcelona and later Paris Saint-Germain Messi's career as an international player was awash with disappointments, near-misses and even heartbreaks on the most prestigious stage. In this section we'll discuss Messi's World Cup journey, exploring his various heartbreak experiences that he's endured, as well as the effect it had on the legacy he left behind.

2006: An Optimistic Start, but a disappointing

Messi's first experience of the World Cup came in 2006 at the age of 18, and he was playing for the first time in 2006. The teen Argentine athlete showed glimpses of his incredible talent, however the tournament ended prematurely because of injury. Argentina advanced to the quarterfinals, but ultimately lost to Germany and left Messi and his fellow Argentinians with a bitter taste of defeat.

2010: A Quarterfinal Final Exit and More Questions about underperformance

2010. The World Cup in South Africa witnessed Messi take on the competition in the role of being one of most thrilling athletes. The tournament, however, was a disappointment again after they were eliminated from the quarterfinals against Germany. Although he scored four goals during the competition, Messi faced criticism for not performing well in important games, further fuelling the notion that he could not duplicate his form at club at the world stage.

2014 2013: An Chance at Glory Slips Away

In 2014, the World Cup held in Brazil offered Messi with the perfect opportunity to take home the ultimate football prize. Messi was the captain of Argentina through to the final showing incredible skill and scoring important goals in the process. In the final, against Germany, Messi was unable to motivate his team to triumph. It ended with losing 1-0 in extra time. It left Messi sad and Argentina in shock. Even though he was awarded the title of tournament's best player but the bitterness of losing was a distraction from his achievements.

2018: Is it the Ende of the Era?

When Messi was preparing for what might be his final chance to win World Cup glory in Russia the expectation was high in his Argentine the national side. But the event proved to be unforgiving for Argentina which was plagued by problems within the team, lack of performance as well as early exit in the round of 16 at the final champions France. Messi looked dejected during the entire tournament, and it appeared as if the pressure of expectation took its toll on him.

Legacy and the Cost of Glory

Messi's World Cup heartbreaks really cast shadows over his stellar career in the era of. While he had a remarkable run for his team but not having the World Cup title was used by critics to devalue his standing as an all-time legend. But it's important to recognize the enormous weight and pressure placed on Messi's shoulders as he carries the nation's aspirations and goals in seeking World Cup glory.

Lionel Messi's World Cup heartbreaks represent a important chapter in his soccer journey. Although he's accomplished almost all of his goals at club level however, his ultimate goal is still elusive when he was playing on an international level. The heartbreaks didn't diminish Messi's extraordinary ability and the happiness the sport has given supporters across the world. Messi's name as one the best players ever to been a part of the sport is immortalized in the record books of history. Messi's World Cup journey serves as an illustration that the path of glory isn't always easy and it's also an indication of his determination and perseverance to push towards success, despite any defeats.

Lionel Messi's Copa America Glory: A Story of Redemption and Triumph

2021 will be remembered in football's history because it was the year that Lionel Messi, the legendary Argentinean forward finally won the international trophy. After a long string of misses and heartbreaks Messi was the one to lead his Argentine the national side to victory at the Copa America, solidifying his standing in the ranks of one of the best players who have played the game with his beautiful touch. In this essay we'll explore the experiences of Messi as well as the Argentine team throughout the competition, focusing on the difficulties they encountered and the joy of their victory, and the significance of this win to Messi's career.

Over the past year, Messi had carried the burden of expectation from his fellow countrymen, despite Argentina having failed to win the major titles in international competitions after in 1993. Copa America. In spite of numerous wins at club level for Barcelona however, many critics complained about the lack of any major award in Messi's career as an international player. It was the 2021 Copa America, hosted by Argentina and Colombia provided Messi the chance to disarm the doubters and fulfill his goal.

Dominance of the Group Stage

Argentina started the Copa America campaign in fine performance, eliminating every opponent in the initial group stage. Messi in the captain's armband showed his skill on the field as he orchestrated the team's attack performance and also demonstrating exceptional skills and a sharp eye. Through assists and goals and goals, he played a major role for Argentina's wins against Chile, Uruguay, and Paraguay. Team's dominating performance in the group stage, not only led them to knockout stages, but also helped to instill an attitude of confidence and a sense of unity in the team.

Knockout Drama

The knockout stage during the Copa America provided some nerve-wracking moments for Argentina as well as their supporters. In the quarterfinals Argentina faced Ecuador in the semi-finals, and despite a strong performance from the Ecuadorian team, Messi's superb free-kick and late goal secured a 3-1 victory for Argentina. In the semifinal match, Colombia was a test of the team's strength in a high-stress penalty shootout. Messi showed nerves of steel by kicking his spot-kick with ease as Argentina won, securing their place in the final with arch-rivals, Brazil.

The Triumph Final

The game against Brazil was of immense importance. Argentina and Brazil have one of the most fierce rivalries in soccer A win over the two teams that are bitter enemies could make the victory extra special for Messi as well as his team. It was a tense match, both sides showing their defensive skills. But it was Argentina that broke the deadlock in the 22nd minute with Angel Di Maria, who made a stunning chip on the Brazilian goalkeeper. The goal sparked joyous scenes among Argentine supporters and players.

In the midst of Messi's calmness and grit, Argentina held firm in defense and fought back Brazilian attack. The whistle that ended the game was the beginning of a riot as Messi and his team-mates celebrated their hard-fought victory. The victory not only ended Argentina's wait of 28 years for an international championship, but also gave Messi with the piece missing to his impressive career.

Lionel Messi's Copa America triumph holds immense importance, not just to him, but for Argentina as well as the entire world of soccer. The win confirms his position as one of the greatest best players and demonstrates his ability to perform on the most prestigious stage. It also highlights the development of Messi in leadership, since the Argentine captain led a gifted however often unbalanced Argentine team to victory by his ability, grit and inspiring leadership.

In addition, this victory will resonate with the Argentine people who regard football as an essential element of their identity as a nation. Messi's victory was a needed cause of happiness and unification during tough moments, reviving the spirit of a nation.

Lionel Messi's Copa America triumph represents the end of his long-running search for glory on the world stage. By demonstrating his remarkable capabilities, leadership and devotion to the game, Messi led Argentina to success in the competition and ended a lengthy streak of trophy-less games and marking his name on the football calendar. The victory not only bolsters Messi's name but also provides enormous joy to his teammates. When the world is celebrating this incredible achievement and celebrates the success of Messi, it is an example of the strength of perseverance as well as the rewards of unwavering commitment.

Chapter 9: The Messi-Ronaldo Rivalry

The battle among Lionel Messi and Cristiano Ronaldo has been a fascination for football fans all over all over the globe for nearly 10 years. Both of them are constantly pushing the boundaries of the game, earning unimaginable success, and even rewriting record books. Beyond individual brilliance the Messi-Ronaldo saga provides lessons on perseverance, determination as well as an obsession for the highest level. In this article we'll dive into the real essence of this battle and the lessons that it can teach us.

The power of Competitiveness:

The Messi-Ronaldo rivalry is a perfect example of the potential of healthy rivalry. The two players constantly push one another to greater goals, fueled by their thirst to be the best. Being present in the field has pushed each other to work to perform better. Their competition has become an incentive to personal development and set the standard for other players playing the game.

This is a lesson that healthy competition is beneficial, not just on the field but also in every area of our lives. If we are surrounded by people who are willing to challenge

We inspire ourselves to be better, so that we can unlock our potential to become the best we've ever thought could be possible.

Divers paths to success:

A fascinating aspect of the rivalry between Messi and Ronaldo is the different styles they play and their personalities. Messi is a model of grace, elegance and finesse. He also has an unparalleled ability to move across defenses with ease. Ronaldo however, on the other is a symbol of the power of athleticism as well as a relentless drive with his athleticism, and frequently uses it to take on his opponents. This divergent approach shows that there's no universal way to be successful.

The key lesson to learn is that accepting our own unique strengths and harnessing your strengths to their maximum will result in extraordinary accomplishments. Messi as well as Ronaldo have demonstrated the importance of self-awareness and honesty. crucial in the pursuit of perfection, at and off the field.

Resilience and resilience in the face of Adversity:

Both Messi as well as Ronaldo were both faced with numerous difficulties throughout their professional careers. From injury to criticism as well as setbacks and losses, they've shown their unflinching resilience even in the face of hardship. They've turned their disappointments into motivation and are constantly working to make improvements and prove doubters to be wrong. The ability of their team to bounce back from adversity exemplifies the value of mental strength as well as a constant focus on achieving one's goals.

This is the lesson to learn that failures and setbacks happen in the world, but it's how we respond to these defeats that define our character. Messi and Ronaldo demonstrate the importance of self-belief, perseverance and never giving up, providing inspiration to get over obstacles and attain excellence.

Teams and leadership:

The Messi-Ronaldo rivalry is often portrayed as a fight between the two however both players have displayed exceptional teamwork and leadership capabilities. They've always elevated the teams they play for, and have inspired their players to do their highest. The play-making skills of Messi and Ronaldo as well as his ability to score crucial goals has made them essential coaches on the pitch.

This is a lesson that brilliance of individuals is amplified when it is paired with leadership and teamwork. No matter what the subject of collaboration, a strong teamwork and the capacity to motivate and unify a group are crucial to achieving success as a team.

Sportmanship and Humility:

While battling their rivalry Messi and Ronaldo showed impressive respect and humility. Even in the midst of intense rivalry and intense rivalry, they've shown the respect they have for each other's skills and successes. Their behavior in and out of the playing field reminds us that greatness can't be solely measured by personal accolades but also how the person is treated.

This is a lesson that sportsmanship and humility are characteristics that transcend individual successes. No matter what our capabilities or achievements, treating people with kindness and respect is an essential part of being a champion.

The Messi-Ronaldo rivalry has surpassed the borders of football and captivated all around the globe with its intensity and sheer brilliance. Beyond their incredible talents and accomplishments This rivalry imparts valuable teachings to those who watch it. From the impact of competitiveness and the necessity of acknowledging the strengths of each individual to perseverance, teamwork and humour, Messi as well as Ronaldo have left a lasting footprint on the field of sports.

Their ongoing battle is a constant reminder that success can be attained by perseverance, determination and the constant determination to achieve excellence. When we are witnessing the closing pages of their legendary careers, we are able to consider the important lessons that were learned from the Messi-Ronaldo saga and take them into our own life, and strive for excellence wherever we choose to take.

Chapter 10: Messi's Humanitarian Work And Personal Life

Lionel Messi is not only the greatest footballer of all time, but also an example of motivation and kindness. His achievements in the game have garnered his fame to the world however, it's crucial to examine his personal life in order to fully discover the person who is who is the man behind his footballing talent. This article focuses on Messi's personal life, which includes his marriage as well as his children and amazing humanitarian initiatives he's been involved in throughout his professional career.

Messi's private Life

The Early Years and the Family Background:

To comprehend Messi's private world It is essential to study his early days. Lionel Andres Messi was born on the 24th of June on the 24th of June, 1987, from Rosario, Argentina. Growing up in a family of modest means his love for soccer was apparent from an early age. The family he was raised in played a crucial contribution to nurturing his talent as well as assisting him in his pursuit of goals.

Love and Marriage Antonela Rocuzzo:

Messi's private life took on another turn after the soccer star was introduced to Antonela Roccuzzo, a childhood crush. The couple began their relationship at the end of their teens, and were married the 30th of June, 2017 in the city of their birth, Rosario. The wedding was an opulent ceremony, which was attended by Messi's soccer colleagues as well as other well-known people.

Family's Role and Fatherhood:

Messi's private life grew when he welcomed three of his children: Thiago, Mateo, and Ciro. Being a father has been an transformative event for Messi who frequently shows his gratitude and love towards his kids. The family he has with him is an anchor of security and love, and provides an oasis in the midst of the pressures of his soccer professional.

The Humanitarian Work of Messi

Leo Messi Foundation: Leo Messi Foundation:

In addition to his remarkable football skills, Messi has consistently used his fame to make a significant impact on the society. He founded his foundation, the Leo Messi Foundation, a foundation that is a charitable organisation dedicated to providing the opportunity to receive education and health care for children who are at risk. The foundation's efforts have helped millions of children around the world, providing children the chance to have a brighter tomorrow.

UNICEF Ambassador:

In the year 2010, Messi became a Goodwill Ambassador for UNICEF which is the United Nations Children's Fund. As a result of this the actor has been active in spreading awareness of the issues that affect children like healthcare, education and social integration. His collaboration with UNICEF has shed some light on the situation of the children in poverty and helped others contribute to their wellbeing.

Medical Initiatives

His charitable endeavors extend to the medical sector also. He financed the development of a Pediatric Cancer Centre in Barcelona which provides children fighting cancer with cutting-edge medical facilities. In addition, he has contributed to various initiatives in medical research, such as helping to build that of the Hospital Sant Joan de Deu located in Barcelona.

Disaster Assistance:

Messi has shown a tremendous amount of kindness and compassion during moments of need. After natural disasters such as the earthquake that struck Haiti in 2010 as well as the flooding in Argentina 2013 Messi gave a significant amount of money in aiding the relief efforts. The aid he provided has been a significant impact on the lives of people suffering from these catastrophes.

Social Effects:

Messi's efforts to help others haven't solely focused on monetary contributions but also creating awareness and encouraging people to take action. His role as a role-model extends far beyond the field of football, inspiring players and fans to take part in charitable endeavors and to contribute to the society.

Lionel Messi's personal life as well as his charitable efforts provide a peek into the personality and beliefs of the man who created the

footballing legend. The love he has for his family and friends, his passion for having a positive effect as well as his unwavering dedication towards improving the lives of children are examples of his remarkable qualities outside the sport. Messi's capability to leverage his platform to bring about significant change is an inspirational example for us all and reminds that we have a profound effect that we have in the world when we combine our passions with genuine compassion for those around us.

Chapter 11: Lionel's Move To Paris Saint-Germain

Lionel Messi's move his team to Paris Saint-Germain (PSG) in the summer of 2021 sounded waves of shock throughout the world of football. After spending the entirety of his professional life at Barcelona the move of Messi to PSG in the French capital was a fresh phase in his long and illustrious career. This article examines Messi's move to PSG and focuses on his impressive results and performances during the 2022 World Cup, where he showed his remarkable talent on the international stage.

Messi's Transfer to Paris Saint-Germain

The Final Day of the Era in Barcelona:

In the midst of more than a decade in Barcelona Messi's departure from the Catalan club shocked fans across the world. The financial strain and the contractual issues resulted in his deportation and the conclusion of a period defined by his incredible record-breaking success as well as numerous achievements in Barcelona. His transfer to PSG marked a significant transformation in the game.

The Paris Saint-Germain Project:

Messi's move to PSG added to the already stellar team that includes players such as of Neymar and Kylian Mbappe. PSG's goal to be a winner of the UEFA Champions League received a major boost after the arrival of Messi, the Argentine superstar. The world of football was eagerly anticipating the sparks and excitement to come from the star-studded trio.

Accepting the new challenges of life:

Messi's switch to PSG demonstrated his capacity to accept new challenges and adjust to a completely different way of playing. The change from Barcelona's possession-oriented game to PSG's direct and offensive approach was a great opportunity for Messi to show his versatility and adaptability in his game.

Messi's Success and Feats in the 2022 World Cup

Record Breaking:

In 2022, the FIFA World Cup held in Qatar provided a stage for Messi to build on his reputation to be one of the most renowned footballers of all time. In the course of the competition, he broke records in every direction by eclipsing the record-breaking World Cup scoring record and becoming the tournament's all time leading assist player. These achievements did not just highlight his brilliance as an individual, but also proved his power in the sport and his capability to inspire the team.

Inspirational Argentina to be a World Champion:

Messi's influence grew beyond his personal records, as he helped lead Argentina to victory at 2022's World Cup. This tournament gave Messi with an opportunity to realize his goal of capturing the trophy alongside his team. His efforts were extraordinary showing a mixture of vision, skill, and the ability to lead. The ability of his to make opportunities, score important goals, and manage the game of his team was a major contributor in Argentina's performance.

The Golden Boot and Tournament Player

Messi's exceptional performances during his time at the World Cup earned him the Golden Boot as the tournament's highest scorer as well as The Player of the Tournament accolade. His achievements went beyond stats because he demonstrated an unmatched comprehension of the game incredible creativity and the unwavering desire to win. His impact upon the Argentina's World Cup triumph was undeniable.

The symbol for National Pride:

Messi's triumph in his victory at the World Cup carried immense significance for Argentina. This victory did not just end an extended drought of trophy wins for

Argentina's national team, but it made Messi a one of the most beloved national heroes. His capacity to unite an entire nation and provide joy to millions of people in Argentina proved his worth beyond football.

Lionel Messi's switch his way to Paris Saint-Germain and his remarkable accomplishments in 2022's World Cup showcased his adaptability as well as his tenacity and ability on the international arena. The move to PSG proved his ability to take on the new challenges that come with it and contribute to the development of a brand new team. When he was at the World Cup, Messi's performances were simply outstanding and he set records while taking Argentina to glory as well as inspiring the nation. Messi's Golden Boot and Player of the Tournament awards were a testimony to his incredible ability and the effect his performance had on the competition.

While Messi continues to leave his mark on Paris Saint-Germain and pursue further achievements in his career, his actions as well as his achievements during the 2022 World Cup will forever be immortalized in the history of football. They are a constant reminder of his incredible talent and ability to surpass the game, capturing the imagination and heart of soccer fans across all over the world.

Chapter 12: Messi's Legacy The Retirement Options After 2023

A Story of Immortality and the Farewell

The year is 2023 The year 2023 in which Lionel Messi stands at the crossing point of his famous career. The Argentine master has dazzled footballers from all over the world for over a decade making an irresistible impression on the game. His talents keep awestruck, questions are raised about the next phase of his career, as well as his final decision on when to retire.

Messi's Legacy:

For a full understanding of the magnitude of Messi's legacy, you must reflect on the influence he's had on football's beautiful game. Beginning with his first years in Barcelona in which he rose to the top at La Masia, to the many trophies, records and personal accolades he earned the greatness of Messi is a constant force in the world of football.

His incredible dribbling abilities sharp vision and a honed-in-the-middle finishing style make him an absolute nightmare for defenses, and an absolute delight to be a part of for fans. Messi's goalscoring records have redefined things that were once believed to be feasible, while his collaboration with Barcelona created a era of supremacy that will remain in the football record books.

His legacy stretches far beyond the court. His sportsmanship, kindness and undying dedication to the game make him an ideal inspiration for players from all over the world. His charitable endeavors, including Leo Messi Foundation Leo Messi Foundation and collaborations with other organizations, such as UNICEF and UNICEF, have enriched the lives of many kids and established his position as a world-renowned ambassador of soccer.

Retirement Options:

In the moment that Messi is nearing the end of his playing career, the decision to quit becomes the subject of discussion and debate. The constant wear and tear of professional football, in conjunction with the physical demands of elite games, have raised questions regarding the length of time he will remain at the top of the game.

One thing is for sure the awe-inspiring skill of Messi and his athletic ability suggest that he can defy the age and keep performing at a high level throughout the years. His capacity to change his style of play, mitigate decline in physical fitness with time and help make a difference in the performance of his squad is a clear indication that retiring could be just a distant idea.

But, the cost of a lengthy and legendary career can't be overlooked. The physical strain, the stress of being constantly scrutinized, and the burden of the expectations of a nation's future will wear down even the strongest athletes. While Messi thinks about retiring, the considerations regarding his future health as well as his family's life and the wish to begin a new phase outside of football could be brought to the fore.

The Finale:

When the moment comes for Messi to say goodbye to the football game that was the foundation of his career for the last decade, it'll be a time of tremendous importance. All football fans are expected to honor one of the best players who have ever graced the field, and feelings will be intense when teammates, fans, and even rivals all bid farewell to an icon.

Messi's departure, however it happens it will be accompanied with a feeling of loss to the sport. His departure will leave an unfilled void that can't be quickly filled. It will also serve as an opportunity to reflect, as football fans celebrate the many memories, the power and brilliance Messi has given throughout his playing career.

When he retires, Messi will have the possibility of shaping his legacy in different ways. Be it by coaching youngsters, or following various other interests, his effect in the sport will never cease to resonate. Additionally, his non-sports contributions as a philanthropist and as a social advocate concerns, will be an affirmation of his character and values the team holds to.

While Lionel Messi navigates the final decades of his illustrious life, his achievements shine brilliantly. In everything from his unparalleled achievements on the field, through his modest manner of life and

charitable endeavors, Messi has set a high standard for excellence that will last for generations. In the end, the decision to retire at any time to pass, is a highly personal choice, with considerations of health, family and the personal fulfillment.

If it is time for Messi to say goodbye the world of football will gather to honor his incredible achievements in the field. Although his loss will be felt however, his legacy will go through the generations to come, inspiring new generations of footballers and informing us of the wonder which can be created with dedication, skill as well as a constant love of football.

Chapter 13: Early Life

Lionel Messi was born on June 24, 1987 within the town of Rosario, Argentina. He was raised in the middle class of his family, at a young time, it became apparent that he was a passionate desire for soccer. His talent was quickly apparent when he started playing football at a club that was local known as "Grandoli" in the age of five.

At age 8years old, Messi began playing in the youth squad at Newell's Old Boys, a very wellknown Argentine football team. His exceptional abilities on the field drew the attention of numerous who noticed him, and soon he started receiving offers from numerous famous clubs. But, when he reached 11 years of age, Messi faced a major defeat. His diagnosis was that he had hormone deficiency, also known as a growth that impacted the physical development of his body.

His talent was not remain unnoticed. At 13 years of age Messi caught the eye of FC

Barcelona's sports director, Carles Rexach. Incredibly impressed by the skills of Messi, Rexach offered him a agreement on napkins, signifying the start of his experience with the legendary club.

In order to provide him with the proper treatment needed to treat his deficiency in growth hormone, Messi and his family had to make the hard decision of moving in Barcelona, Spain. He enrolled at Barcelona's Youth Academy, La Masia, where the academy provided specialized education and assistance in his physical growth.

Despite initial difficulties, Messi quickly adjusted to his new environment, and continued to shine in the field. Messi climbed through the junior groups in Barcelona with a remarkable talent and incredible performance. In the nick of time, he made his first appearance in the team at age 17 and became the youngest player to ever sport Barcelona's iconic jersey.

His extraordinary abilities, quickness and goalscoring abilities quickly became a global phenomenon. His fame grew as one of the best young talents all while enthralling fans and making opponents awestruck of his talents. The struggles of his childhood and the determination to overcome obstacles made his career into the legendary footballer that he is today.

BIRTH AND CHILDHOOD

Lionel Messi was born into an intimate family from Rosario, Argentina. His parents include Jorge Messi and Celia Cuccittini. Messi is the older brother of two, Rodrigo and Matias, along with a sibling, Maria Sol. While growing up, the family of Messi was a major influence in his life, and encouraged Messi in his pursuit of football aspirations.

Messi's love for football was heavily influenced and shaped by his parents. The father of his son, Jorge employed as an industrial steelworker, and was also a coach parttime. Jorge saw Lionel's incredible ability from a very early stage and played an important part in encouraging and supporting the development of his soccer skills.

Messi's mom, Celia, worked in an industrial workshop for the manufacture of magnets. She was an unconditional source of affection and encouragement to Lionel during his soccer matches and helping him face the obstacles he encountered during his first professional career. Messi frequently expressed gratitude at his mother and father for their constant assistance and for their part in influencing his road to achieve his goals.

Family has always been a solid source of support in the life of Messi throughout his professional career. He's known for his modesty and grounded personality and is usually due to the morals that were instilled into him through his parents. While he has achieved global recognition and fame, Messi has always maintained an intimate relationship with his family members, often showing his appreciation and love for the influence they have had in his life.

Alongside his immediate family members, Messi is a fatherly guy himself. He was married to his childhood sweetheart, Antonela Roccuzzo, in 2017. They have been friends with one another since they were extremely young. They now have three children: Thiago, Mateo, and Ciro.

FAMILY AND UPBRINGING

His upbringing and the role of his family members in his life had a huge impact on developing his character and how he responds to football. Family support and affection are a major factor in his development into one of the best soccer players ever.

Introduction to Football

His introduction to football came at an early young age. Born on the 24th of June 1987 at Rosario, Argentina, Messi started to play football when he was just five. It was apparent from the beginning that he was a natural ability and passion for football.

Messi's enthusiasm to play football was fostered by his extended family, particularly his mother, Celia. Celia saw his talent and was a fervent advocate for his soccer dreams. When she was eighteen, Messi joined the youth team of Newell's Old Boys, a wellknown Argentine soccer club that was based in the city of his birthplace, Rosario.

In his time playing at Newell's Old Boys that Messi's remarkable skills and capabilities began to show their true potential. His agility, speed, and incredible dribbling ability attracted the attention of both coaches and fans alike. Messi's impressive performances with Newell's Old Boys soon drew an interest from elite clubs and both in Argentina as well as abroad.

At 11 years old, Messi got a major break after he was approached by FC Barcelona's director of sports, Carles Rexach. In Argentina, Rexach saw Messi playing for a local team and was awed by the talent of his player. Impressed by his skills, Rexach immediately offered him an agreement with Barcelona.

Due to budgetary constraints as well as a lack of documentation that was in order this contract was unable to be signed at the time. But, Rexach did not want to let go of Messi's incredible talents and potential. In order to guarantee Messi's acceptance in the future, he wrote his contract on a napkin, as an expression of his commitment and confidence in the teen superstar.

The year 2003 was the time that Messi as well as his wife decided of moving in Barcelona, Spain, to continue his career in football. The move enabled Messi to be a part of Barcelona's highly regarded young academy La Masia, where the academy would provide worldclass coaching and also receive a highquality education. La Masia, known for its emphasis on the development of technical skills and nurturing the next generation of talent it proved to be an ideal environment for Messi to develop his talents.

under the direction of skilled coaches as well as gifted players, Messi thrived in La Masia's competitive and structured atmosphere. Messi showed his outstanding talents and swiftly rose up his ranks, and capturing the attention of players and coaches with his impressive performances.

The football debut of Messi did not just allow him to showcase his extraordinary abilities, but it also signified the start of his path to becoming among the best footballers ever. The early years of his career laid the basis for his unforgettable career which was characterized by numerous recordbreaking performances, individual accolades as well as a huge amount of success at both international and club level. Lionel Messi's first encounter with football was the catalyst that led to a tale of talent determination, commitment, and unmatched success in football. It is a beautiful sport.

3. RISE to STARDOM

Lionel Messi's meteoric rise to fame is a thrilling adventure that demonstrates his remarkable ability, determination, and determination. As a child it was clear that Messi was a footballer with extraordinary talent, and the path to fame began.

His talent first became apparent when he was a part of the young group at Newell's Old Boys, a wellknown Argentine soccer club aged just eight. His abilities in the field were unparalleled as he soon became the mainstay of the team. At the age of 11 Messi suffered a significant problem when he was diagnosed the growth hormone shortage and it affected the growth of his body and physique.

In spite of this his talent didn't remain unnoticed. In 2003, he drew the eye of FC Barcelona's sports director, Carles Rexach, during the course of a test in the club. The director was impressed with Messi's abilities, Rexach offered him a agreement on napkins which was a symbol of friendship which marked the start of Messi's career with Barcelona.

To supply Messi with the proper treatment for the deficiency of his growth hormone His family took the choice of moving into Barcelona, Spain. Messi was accepted into Barcelona's academy for youth, La Masia, where the academy provided specialized training as well as assistance for his physical growth. Through his time at the academy Messi was able to keep his place in the spotlight as he rose up through the ranks thanks to his incredible talents and achievements.

At 17 years old, Messi made his firstteam debut with Barcelona and became the youngest player ever to take part at an official game. The debut of Messi was only the beginning of his impressive career. Messi quickly became the most important player at Barcelona as he captivated fans and pundits in the field with his amazing agility, dribbling and scoring abilities.

Over the course of his career his performances in the field are extraordinary. He's broken many records, received numerous awards for team and individual and has established new standards for excellence in football. The incredible consistency of Messi and his capacity to be a hero in the most crucial of instances have earned him praise among the most outstanding players in history.

His meteoric rise to fame is proof of his unwavering devotion as well as his hardworking enthusiasm for the game. The journey of Messi isn't just an inspiration to young players, but also a testimony to the strength of determination and the ability. Messi's accomplishments both on and off the pitch are a testament to his status in the football world and become an icon for millions of football fans across the globe.

Chapter 14: Joining Fc Barcelona Academy

Lionel Messi joined the FC Barcelona youth academy, La Masia, at the age of thirteen. The move marked a major change in his career and established the basis for his extraordinary journey with the club.

The talent of Messi had already attracted the attention of Barcelona's sport director Carles Rexach, when Messi was only eleven years old. Due to financial limitations and worries concerning his lack of growth hormone An official invitation from Barcelona was pushed back.

The year 2003 was the time that Messi as well as his loved ones took the decision to move in Barcelona, Spain, to offer him the best chance to get the treatment he needed to treat his illness. Barcelona offered the medical assistance and growth hormone treatments which Messi was in need of.

When he moved from Barcelona, Messi officially joined La Masia, the renowned youth academy run by the club. La Masia has gained a fame as being among the top soccer schools in the world recognized for its ability to nurture youngsters and focusing on technological development.

With the help of skilled and committed coaches from La Masia, Messi continued to develop his talents and improve as a player. The academy was a highly structured setting in which Messi was able to train intensely and improve his skills.

While at his academy Messi advanced through different youth teams and showed his incredible ability, ball control and dribbling abilities. He was a standout among other players and showed consistently extraordinary performances in the court.

His dedication to his sport, in conjunction with the training and support that he received from La Masia, earned him rapid transfer to Barcelona's main team. When he was 17 Messi made his debut with the first team The rest is the story.

The FC Barcelona youth academy was an important move in the development of Lionel Messi's career. It gave him the opportunity to improve his abilities as well as receive specific training and develop as a footballer. La Masia's experience La Masia equipped him with the required tools for success at the top level and laid the groundwork to his tremendous success with FC Barcelona.

Youth Career Achievement

The achievements of Lionel Messi throughout his young career are an ode to his extraordinary ability and potential in the field of football. There are some noteworthy achievements during his formative years:

1. Recordbreaking Goal Scorer Messi showed his skill in goal scoring from a very young age. In 2003 and 2004, in Barcelona's youth squad the player scored 36 goals over just 30 matches, which set records for most goals scored in one year in the Barcelona youth team.

2. FIFA U20 World Cup Triumph in 2005. Messi played for Argentina at the FIFA U20 World Cup held in the Netherlands. He was a key player in aiding Argentina to win the tournament scoring six goals while assisting with numerous goals. Messi's performance earned an award of the FIFA World Youth Championship Golden Ball that is given to the player who performed best during the competition.

3. The youngest Barcelona player: Messi made his firstteam debut with FC Barcelona in a friendly game with FC Porto in November 2003 aged 16 years and 140 days. He was the shortest player ever to be a part of Barcelona in a match that was officially sanctioned.

4. Scores at scoring in the Champions League: At the age of 17 and 218 yrs, Messi became the youngest scoring player ever to score in the UEFA Champions League. Messi found the net for Panathinaikos in December of 2005, showing off his goalscoring skills at the top level of European soccer.

5. Golden Boy Award: In 2005, Messi received the prestigious Golden Boy award, recognizing him as the top athlete in the midst of European football. The accolade also highlighted the extraordinary performance of his team and their his potential as a future star.

The early successes laid the groundwork for Messi's remarkable career. They also provided a glimpse into the glory that was to arrive. These achievements showcased his extraordinary capabilities, as well as his maturation beyond age, and laid the scene for his rise to be one of the best footballers of all time.

Promotion to the Senior Team

Lionel Messi's move to FC Barcelona's senior side was an extremely anticipated and important milestone in his career. His exceptional talent and achievements on the youth team stood out as a star player who was that was destined to be a star, and he caught the notice of his teammates, coaches as well as the fans.

Messi's meteoric rise in Barcelona's academy for youth, La Masia, showcased the immense talent and potential of this player. As he continued his rise and develop in his game and develop as a player, it became apparent that he was ready to take the next stage that of being a part of the team's senior squad.

The pivotal moment occurred on October 16th, 2004, the day that Messi made his first official appearance with FC Barcelona's inaugural team, at 17. The coach Frank Rijkaard, recognizing Messi's extraordinary talents, gave Messi the chance to demonstrate his worth in a match against Espanyol. Messi made his debut as a substitute during the 87th minute to replace Deco He immediately displayed his dazzling dribbling abilities and speed on the field. Even though he played only just a couple of minutes but his influence was evident.

The debut was an insight into Messi's vast potential, and left football fans as well as pundits amazed by his talents. Despite being only a few years old, Messi showcased his fearlessness of character, grit, and the ability to handle seasoned players easily. His appearance and performance as a senior player confirmed the place he was in Barcelona's squad.

Through the entire 20042005 campaign, Messi made appearances as an alternate in various games, such as La Liga and the UEFA Champions League. His reputation was established for being a player who has incredible technical capabilities, a quick dribbling and a keen eye on goals.

The following seasons his role in the following seasons was growing and his contribution to the squad became more evident. His incredible dribbles and precise passing, and goalscoring skills helped to make a significant contribution to the success of Barcelona. Messi made formidable alliances with his fellow stars Ronaldinho, Samuel Eto'o, as well as, later on, Andres Iniesta and Xavi Hernandez. They created one of the greatest soccer teams of all time.

The promotion of Messi to the team's senior ranks led to the dawn of a new age of greatness for both him and Barcelona. He was a master of his craft, Messi went on to perform incredible feats. These included winning several awards, breaking records and achieving individual awards including the prestigious Ballon d'Or award.

Promotion of Messi into the team's senior ranks was a great move by Barcelona. This gave him a opportunity to show his talents at the top levels in professional soccer. With his outstanding performance Lionel Messi would ascend to being one of the most outstanding footballers ever and leave an imprint on football.

4. Career in Football

Lionel Messi's career in football has been nothing less than extraordinary. Beginning with his time with FC Barcelona to his current position as an iconic figure in football, Messi has consistently showcased his incredible talent, versatility and determination to succeed. We'll look at the most important moments of his remarkable career.

Beginning Years with FC Barcelona:

His professional journey began at FC Barcelona, where he made his debut in the club's first team in 2004and became the youngest player in history to be a part of Barcelona at that time. Due to his incredible dribbling abilities as well as his closeball control and a dazzling ability to see, Messi swiftly became a crucial player in Barcelona's success under the direction of legendary coaches such as Frank Rijkaard and Pep Guardiola.

Unprecedented Success in Barcelona:

Through the years, Messi played a pivotal part in the dominance of Barcelona in both domestic as well as international level. Alongside his stalwart teammates like Andres Iniesta, and Xavi Hernandez, Messi was the foundation of the team. They won many La Liga titles, Copa del Rey trophy, as well as even the UEFA Champions League multiple times. Under the tutelage of Guardiola and guidance, Messi's impact in the game grew more and he was an integral member of the renowned Barcelona team, which is famous for its offensive, possessionbased approach to football.

Recordbreaking Individual Achievements and Records

The individual achievements of Messi are just more impressive than his team's accomplishments. He has received the famous FIFA Ballon d'Or award multiple times, making him one of the best footballers of all time. From 2009 until in 2012 Messi made history as the very first footballer to be awarded the Ballon d'Or four consecutive times. His playing ability and scoring abilities have helped him set many records, including the highest number of goals he has scored in one calendar year.

Transfer from Paris SaintGermain (PSG):

After playing his whole professional life in Barcelona, Messi transferred to Paris SaintGermain (PSG) due to financial issues that his previous club was facing. This was an exciting move and opened a new chapter in the storied career of Messi. Although it's still too early to evaluate his achievements in the club of PSG however his contribution will be substantial and he will form a formidable trio alongside Neymar as well as Kylian Mbappe.

International Careers:

The contributions of Messi to his contribution to Argentine the national side are meritorious. In spite of a few controversies early throughout his international career Messi was able to lead Argentina to a win in important events. The year 2021 was the time Messi achieved his first international prize by winning the Copa America with the national team. It was the fulfillment of his efforts to win the highest honors for his nation, and solidified his place as one of Argentina's most renowned footballers.

Legacy and Impact:

Lionel Messi's contribution to his sport is far more than recordbreaking achievements and awards. Messi has redefined expectations for players, and combines extraordinary skill, agility and an innate footballing intelligence. His longevity and consistency in the most elite of levels has awed both experts and fans alike. He is often praised as the next generation of football legends such as Diego Maradona and Pele, Messi has earned his own spot within the ranks of legendary footballers.

In the end, Lionel Messi's career in football is an example of his extraordinary talent, determination to excellence, and impressive achievements. From his beginnings at Barcelona before his departure to PSG the club, he's left an imprint on football, enthralling all over the world through his amazing performance. His legacy as one of the best players of all time has been well established, and his legacy will be felt by generations to be.

Chapter 15: Record-Breaking Seasons

Lionel Messi's recordbreaking seasons shown his incredible ability and perseverance on the field of football. Through his entire time in the game, Messi has shattered numerous records and established new standards and left a lasting impression on the game. Here's a look back at his greatest recordbreaking seasons

20112012 Season:

The season of 20112012 was an exceptional season for Messi. He broke records for the highest number of goals scored in one European club season. He scored the astonishing number of 73 goals in every competition. This record breaking feat beat earlier records of 67 goals set by Gerd Mueller in the 19721973 season. Messi's goalscoring prowess was instrumental in helping Barcelona achieve their La Liga title and achieve victory at the Copa del Rey.

2012. Calendar Year 2012:

In the wake of his impressive performances in the season 20112012, Messi carried his goalscoring achievements into 2012. He set yet another record with the recordbreaking 91 goals within the span of a calendar year. The record was higher than the previous record set by Gerd Mueller back in 1972. It was truly a historic achievement, bringing Messi his FIFA Ballon d'Or and cementing his place among the top goal scorers of all time.

20142015 Season:

In the 20142015 football season, Messi continued to dazzle and set yet another record. Messi became the top goal scorer in the time of La Liga, surpassing Telmo Zarra's previous record for 251 goal. His consistent scoring style has helped Barcelona achieve their La Liga, Copa del Rey and UEFA Champions League titles, the club achieving a historic triple for the club.

The 20172018 season: Messi's performance throughout the 20172018 campaign demonstrated his consistency and excellence.

He hit another recordbreaking landmark. Messi became the first footballer to make 100 goals during the UEFA Champions League, reaching the milestone in the match against Chelsea in round 16. The record demonstrates Messi's endurance at the top of European soccer.

20202021 Season:

Even though this season was marred with a myriad of difficulties and disruptions because of the COVID19 epidemic, Messi still managed to record records. In March of 2021, he overtook Pele to achieve the record for the footballer with the most goals scored by one club. This feat was accomplished through his 644th goals for Barcelona and erased Pele's lengthy record set by Santos.

This is just one of the recordsbreaking seasons Lionel Messi has had throughout his playing career. Every season has seen him challenge boundaries and record books and astonish the fans with his amazing talent and ability to score goals. Messi's constant drive for perfection has enabled him to make a lasting impression on football and cement his status as a football icon.

ACHIEVEMENT WITH FC Barcelona

Lionel Messi's accomplishments with FC Barcelona are nothing short of extraordinary. In his short time with FC Barcelona, Messi has amassed an numerous list of prizes and personal accolades, which have established him to be one of the top athletes in the history of football. We will look at the achievements he has made at FC Barcelona:

La Liga Titles:

Messi has been a major element of Barcelona's success throughout La Liga. He has been awarded the Spanish league championship on a number of occasions. These include the 20042005, 20052006 20082009, 20092010and 20102011 20122013, 20142015 20172018, 20152016 and the 20182019 season. His outstanding performances and goal scoring ability have played an important part in the dominance of Barcelona in Spanish soccer.

UEFA Champions League Titles:

Messi was instrumental to Barcelona's victories during his role in winning the UEFA Champions League. He was the main force behind Barcelona's attack, Barcelona won the prestigious European club tournament several times. They won the trophy during the 20052006, 20092010, 20102011 and 20142015 seasons. They formed powerful team under the direction of coaches such as Pep Guardiola, and Luis Enrique.

Copa del Rey Titles:

Messi's achievements in the national cup tournaments are impressive too. He's helped Barcelona to win the Copa del Rey, the top Spanish domestic cup repeatedly. The team won the cup in the years 20082009, 20112012 and 20142015 seasons, as well as the 20152016 the 20162017 and 20172018 seasons in which Messi usually playing a crucial contribution to these wins.

Individual Accolades:

His individual accomplishments with Barcelona have been equally impressive. He's won the famous FIFA Ballon d'Or award (now divided in The Best FIFA Men's Player as well as the Ballon d'Or) multiple times in Barcelona's Barcelona jersey. This includes winning this prestigious award in the years 2009, 2010 2011 2011, 2012, 2015 and 2019.

Furthermore, Messi has been the most prolific scorer in La Liga multiple times, winning his prize, the Pichichi Trophy. Also, he has won the European Golden Shoe (given to the highest goalscoring player within European leagues) multiple times, the evidence of his amazing goalscoring skills. Messi's achievements as a player for Barcelona have brought many individual accolades and recordbreaking performances, cementing his status as one of the top players in football.

The Overall Impact

Messi's accomplishments in his time at FC Barcelona go beyond the distinctions and awards he has received individually. His unique approach to play, hypnotic scoring abilities have won the attention of football fans around the world. He's left an irresistible impression on the team, changing the expectation of attackers through his incredible capability to generate and score goals.

The achievements of Lionel Messi at FC Barcelona have been nothing other than remarkable. His role in the club's growth, both on the individual level and as a team and have established his position as a legend in the game. Messi will be forever recognized as Barcelona's greatest players, and his contribution to the club will be remembered

throughout the history of football.

INVESTMENT CAREER INTERNATIONAL With ARGENTINA'S

Lionel Messi's time in the international arena in Argentina has been one filled with extremes and lows that culminated with a historic victory. Even though his achievement at the club level for FC Barcelona is widely celebrated however, his contribution in his role in the Argentine national team should not be ignored. In this article, we will discuss his career in international football:

Initial Stages as well Copa America 2007:

The player made his debut with the Argentina as a player for the national team in the year 2005 when he was just the age of 18. He immediately showed his incredible potential, however success at the world stage was difficult in the beginning of his professional career. In 2007 Messi was a participant at the Copa America, where Argentina ended up as runnersup. Although they didn't win the cup his performances looked promising showing his potential to excel at a high standard.

World Cup 2014 Final:

One of the major highlights of Messi's career as a player was his run towards finals in the FIFA World Cup final in 2014. Messi was a key player in steering the team towards the finals, showing his exceptional leadership skills and talent. Even though Argentina ended up falling short of the goal and lost against Germany at the end of Messi's efforts have earned him his the Golden Ball award for the most outstanding player of the tournament.

Copa America Heartbreaks:

In the years before his final triumph, Messi faced several heartbreaking moments during his time in the Copa America. Argentina made it to the final stage of the Copa America three times during Messi's time in 2007, 2015 and in 2016 yet narrowly failed to win the trophy in each of them. This disappointment was a huge blow for Messi and his country, accelerating the need to win a significant international trophy.

Copa America 2021 Victory:

Messi's career in international football reached its peak in 2021 as Argentina won the Copa America. This tournament was an important moment in the life of Messi as well as his contribution to the Argentina national team. He was a key player in leadership and an athlete, leading Argentina to victory thanks to his ability to score goals and playing skills. His success at the Copa America ended Argentina's 28year trophyless drought, and brought immense happiness to Messi and all of Argentina.

AllTime Top Scorer for Argentina:

Messi has also made his name on Argentine soccer record books as the most prolific goal scorer of the national team. Messi surpassed the record set by Gabriel Batistuta of 54 goals back in 2016 and continues to add goals to his total. Messi's goalscoring exploits in Argentina show his capability to be consistent at the highest level on international stages and boost the overall performance of the team.

Chapter 16: The Overall Impact

Although Messi's career in international football has been criticized and subjected to scrutiny in the past, his dedication and love for the game of Argentina have not diminished. His leadership and performances have played a major role in developing the brand identity of the team as well as creating a new generation of Argentine players. The team's success at this year's Copa America 2021, he has fulfilled his dream of a lifetime

Dream of winning a major trophy for Argentina and establishing his place as one of Argentina's legendary players.

To conclude, Lionel Messi's career as an international player for Argentina has seen a combination of uncertainty, determination and success. From the beginning of setbacks, to making the World Cup final and finally winning victory with the Copa America trophy, Messi's experience is one of determination and determination. His contribution to the national team, both as an athlete and coach, have left a lasting impression on Argentine football's history. They also has elevated his standing as one of the best ever players.

5. Challenges and Triumph

Lionel Messi's life as a player of the game is full of victories and struggles, which have helped shape his image into the legendary one who he is now. We will look at the obstacles he's faced as well as the amazing achievements of his playing career.

Challenges:

1. Physical limitations: Messi faced a significant problem due to his diminutive height, believing that it would hinder his chances for his success. But he fought through this hurdle with his extraordinary skill, speed, and speed.

2. Health issues: In the year the year 2006 Messi faced a huge problem after he was diagnosed with an insufficiency in growth hormone. It required expensive medical

treatments however Barcelona recognised his potential and provided all the assistance needed. Messi's resilience and perseverance through this time of struggle enabled him to pursue his ambitions.

3. High Expectations: Since a very young stage of his life, Messi was hyped as the next superstar for Argentine football. The burden of expectation on his shoulders at the age of just 18 was enormous, yet his performance was always impressive and he consistently delivered exceptional performance.

4. National Team Critics: Despite his enormous success at club at the club level, Messi faced criticism regarding his performance in his Argentine nation's team. In the race to be a winner of the international championship continued to be a huge challenge during his entire career. This led to instances of uncertainty and criticism.

Triumphs:

1. Many titles with Barcelona: Messi enjoyed tremendous successes in his time with FC Barcelona, winning numerous La Liga titles, Copa del Rey title, and UEFA Champions League titles. His role was pivotal in the dominance of Barcelona both locally as well as in Europe and abroad, owing to the ability to score goals as well as his playmaking abilities as well as his leadership.

2. Individual Recognition: Messi has amassed a numerous individual awards that include seven Ballon d'Or titles. These awards honor Messi as one of the top players around the globe and establish his position among the best players of all time.

3. Recordbreaking accomplishments: Messi has shattered various records in his entire career. He was Barcelona's alltime leading scoring player, broke the record for goals scored during a calendar year and has beat numerous other records that affirm his extraordinary ability on the pitch.

4. Copa America 2021 Triumph: One of the most memorable moments in Messi's professional career was when Messi took Argentina to victory at the Copa America, their first significant trophy at international level since 1993. The victory silenced those who had doubts about his accomplishment on the international stage and brought a great feeling of satisfaction to both Messi as well as his country.

5. Personal Development and Leadership Despite the difficulties and pressures faced by him, Messi exhibited incredible personal improvement and maturity over the course of his playing career. He became an effective leader both as well off the field by guiding and motivating players with his passion determination, hard work ethic and the ability to be humble.

Overcoming Physical Obstructions

Lionel Messi's capability to over come physical barriers is a unique element of his life. Despite his small stature He has defied all expectations and earned himself the title of one of the best soccer players in history. Let's look at the way Messi was able to overcome physical barriers:

1. The ability and skill of Messi's extraordinary technique and skills helped him overcome the physical limitations he perceived. The low weight of his body and his speedy rapid acceleration, acrobatics and precise ball control provided him with a significant advantage over the opposition. Messi's ability of dribbling past several defenders while navigating in tight spaces proved his mastery of the ball, as well as his capacity to overcome physical barriers.

2. His balance and agility: stability and agility played an important factor in his accomplishment. His speed at which he changes the direction of his movement, shift his weight and keep his balance when moving at a high rate makes the player extremely difficult to take on. This ability lets him navigate through tight areas, avoid opponents

and keep his cool when faced with oneonone challenges.

3. Tempo and acceleration: While not often praised for speeds, Messi possesses explosive acceleration that allows him to easily leave the defenders to follow. Short, swift sprints and bursts of pace at short distances have regularly taken opponents by surprise and allowed his to open scoring chances for his team and himself. His acceleration burst helps to cover any apparent absence of speed.

4. Football Intelligence: Messi's remarkable soccer intelligence has played a major role in overcoming physical limits. The ability of Messi to analyze the game, anticipate movement and quickly make decisions can allow him to make use of weaknesses in defenses and generate scoring opportunities. Because he is always an inch ahead of his opponent's mental game, Messi maximizes his effectiveness when on the field, and helps make the most of any physical weaknesses.

5. Flexibility and Adaptability The versatility of Messi's player is also a factor in his ability to overcome physical challenges. Though he's predominantly a midfielder attacking or forward, he's shown the capability to excel in a range of positions, adjusting his style of play to meet the needs of his team. If he's playing in the false nine, central playmaker or Winger, his versatility has given him the ability to create areas on the field that the ability to use his talents to the fullest extent.

6. Physical Conditioning: Although he is physically active, Messi has consistently maintained top physical fitness throughout his entire career. Focusing on fitness, strength and endurance have allowed him to handle the demands on his body during soccer and lessen the chance of injury. A commitment to fitness has helped him overcame physical obstacles and compete continuously at a high level.

In the end, Lionel Messi's capacity to conquer physical barriers stems from an extraordinary combination of skill and agility, as well as balance, soccer intelligence, adaptability and a commitment to physical fitness. His exceptional skill set and knowledge of the game has allowed him to succeed despite physical challenges, showing that the success of football cannot be determined solely by physical size, but rather by intelligence, talent, and ability to adapt. Messi's achievements serve as a model for future players, showing that dedication effort, perseverance, and an grasp of the game will allow you to overcome physical limitations and attain excellence.

How to deal with media pressure

Lionel Messi has had to face intense pressure from media throughout his professional career. Here are some of the methods he's dealt with the pressure:

1. Focusing: Messi is known for his ability to keep his focus on his game, despite the media craze that surrounds his. He is well aware of

not letting pressure from outside hinder his game.

2. Insisting on critics: Messi has made a conscious effort to not pay attention to any criticism that is not needed in the media. He concentrates on his sport and does not let criticism or criticism keep him away from his objectives.

3. A solid team Messi has a great team of support from his teammates as well as his family and friends close to him. They give him the support he needs and helps keep him grounded in the face of press scrutinization.

4. Maintaining a lowprofile: Messi is known to have his profile relatively minimal on the field. He steers clear of situations that could be controversial and prefers privacy to avoid the attention of media and keep the sense of calm in his private life.

5. Making use of media for his benefit using media to his advantage Messi might not be a fan of every aspect of the attention media pay

but he has utilized it in his favor when needed. He takes care to decide the best time and place to interact with media outlets, making sure that his comments are properly considered and leave an impact.

As a summary, Lionel Messi copes with the pressure of media by staying in focus on his game, not allowing himself to be criticized as well as having a strong network of supporters, keeping an unassuming appearance as well as using the media to the advantage of his. These tactics have allowed him to deal with the difficulties of getting noticed and still achieving his best at the soccer field.

Lionel Messi's career as an elite footballer was full of challenges as well as victories. At a very young age, Messi faced numerous obstacles however his skill determination, determination and perseverance allowed him to overcome the obstacles and reach a dazzling level of success. Here's a look at the triumphs and challenges Lionel Messi has experienced throughout his professional career.

Challenges:

1. Growth Hormone Deficiency kid, Messi was diagnosed with an insufficient production of growth hormone and this impeded the physical development of his. It meant that he was forced endure expensive medical treatment and move to Argentina in Barcelona, Spain, to take part in FC Barcelona's famed youth academy La Masia.

2. Early Career Challenges: Messi had to face challenges during his beginning career when trying to make himself a permanent fixture as a member of his place in the Barcelona First team. He was competing with experienced players to earn spots in the starting team, while injuries caused challenges. However, his determination and commitment helped him get an enviable spot within the squad.

3. Pressure and Expectations: Since an early age, Messi was hailed as an extraordinary

talent. He was also drew the comparisons of football legends. The pressure was immense and high expectations on Messi's shoulders. Yet, Messi managed to handle the stress with aplomb and delivered consistently exceptional performance.

Triumphs:

1. Unprecedented Achievements with FC Barcelona: Messi enjoyed incredible successes with FC Barcelona, winning numerous local and international championships. Messi was a major contributor to the success of the club with the ability to score goals with aplomb along with his skills at playmaking as well as his leadership on the field.

2. Recordbreaking Achievements Messi broke records across his career. Among them were the highest number of goals scored in an entire calendar year, highest number of goals during the European club season and many goals in the same club. This incredible feat made him one of the top goalscorers of all time in the history of football.

3. Individual Awards: Messi has consistently been recognized with highprofile individual awards which include several FIFA Ballon d'Or titles and European Golden Shoes. The awards recognize his outstanding talents and his contributions to soccer.

4. The triumph of The Argentine National Team: After suffering a number of disappointments while playing for the team of Argentina, Messi finally achieved a important international success when he won the Copa America in 2021. This win ended the drought of trophies in Argentina and was the most memorable moment of Messi's career in international football.

5. Individual Growth and Philanthropy Beyond the football field, Messi has shown immense personal development and has utilized his position to support charitable initiatives. Messi founded Leo Messi Foundation. Leo Messi Foundation, which provides access to education as well as healthcare for the most vulnerable children.

As a conclusion, Lionel's career has served as a testimony to his capability to face the odds and accomplish remarkable victories. Beginning with early struggles as well as physical hurdles to aweinspiring achievement at club level before finally winning in his Argentine National team. Messi's life is one of perseverance with talent and determination, as well as a commitment to the sport which he is passionate about.

Chapter 17: Life Lessons Taught From Lionel Messi

"PASSION"

One of the main life lessons we can pick up by studying Lionel Messi is the importance of enthusiasm. Messi's love for the game is evident throughout every game he takes part in. He truly loves football and this passion motivates Messi to always improve his game and become a better player.

Passion is vital as it drives the motivation and drive. It provides us with the motivation to reach our goals, and conquer difficulties in the process. Messi's commitment to his game is an example of the force of enthusiasm.

Within our life, fostering a strong love for something can result in fulfillment and the achievement. It doesn't matter if it's a pastime as a job, a passion or an issue, choosing something that we are passionate about and trust can give us immense happiness and fulfillment.

In addition, it helps us overcome challenges. Messi was a victim of many challenges throughout his career, which included injuries, and even tough losses However, his enthusiasm for football never ceases. He is stronger than ever and performs with a high level. The strength of his character is a crucial teaching point for all of us Never stop and continue to push ahead, no matter how difficult things become difficult.

The end result is that Messi's enthusiasm for football has taught us to seek out and find what really ignites our souls. When we are pursuing our passions, we are able to live happier lives, combat adversity and accomplish our dreams.

DEDICATION,

One of the primary lessons that we can take from Lionel Messi is dedication. In his long life, Messi has shown an indefinable dedication to his work as well as a remarkable determination to succeed.

The dedication of Messi is evident through his constant determination to be the best on the soccer field. At a very young age He displayed an incredible love for the sport and was eager to dedicate the time of work and instruction to develop his abilities. He continuously strives to improve, always looking for ways to improve his techniques and improve on his capabilities.

The dedication extends far beyond personal accomplishments. Messi is recognized for his teamfocused approach and always placing the team's achievement above individual accolades. Messi is aware of how important it is to work with his team members and strives to be a part of team success. his team.

On the field His dedication to the game is obvious. He lives a disciplined life and focuses on his fitness level, diet and mental wellbeing. The level of dedication he has to his work will allow him to be in the best way he can consistently.

What we can gain from Messi's determination to achieve greatness is that you must put forth constant effort and the determination to push the limits. No matter what our objectives be it in sports, or other aspects of our lives, giving completely to what we love and constantly striving to improve will allow us to accomplish amazing achievements.

HARD work

One of the key life lessons that we can take by studying Lionel Messi is the value of dedication. In his long professional career, Messi has demonstrated an unbeatable work ethic, which has been a key factor in his accomplishments.

His journey to become one of the most successful soccer players of all time wasn't easy. Although he faced physical struggles during his early career, he didn't allowed it to stop him from following his dream. Instead, he took on working hard as a method to get over obstacles and realize the fullest potential.

The dedication of Messi to his training is legend. He is always putting in endless hours at the field of training and is constantly looking for ways to increase his performance and improve his techniques. He recognizes that just talent isn't enough. It is the blend of determination and talent that makes him stand out.

In addition, Messi's devotion to dedication extends far beyond football. Messi is renowned for his discipline, professionalism and drive. He is committed to taking care of the body with regular nutrition, rest and recovery to ensure that he's always physically and mentally in top shape. His determination and mental strength can be seen in his ability to rebound from defeats and push ahead.

What we can take away from Messi's work ethic is that the success of a team cannot be attained overnight. It takes consistent determination, persistence and the determination to do the extra mile. In sports, or in any other field working hard is essential to unlock the full potential of us and reaching our objectives. Messi's life story is an example to all of us and reminds us that with perseverance, everything can be achieved.

PERSEVERANCE IN THE PRESENT of ADVERSITY

One of the most inspirational life lessons we can gain from Lionel Messi is the importance of resilience in the face of challenges. In his professional life, Messi has encountered numerous difficulties and setbacks. But Messi has demonstrated the capacity to bounce back and push forward.

At a very young age, Messi faced physical limitations due to a hormone growth deficit. But, rather than let this stop him from pursuing his goals to become a pro soccer player and a professional athlete, he fought. The doctor treated him and worked hard to improve his game, and never let his physical or height size hinder his progress.

Furthermore, Messi has faced setbacks and defeats on the field too. When it comes to losing crucial games, suffering from injuries or being criticized, Messi has consistently shown the strength and perseverance. The player uses setbacks to serve as motivation to continue improving and show his worth every time.

The perseverance of Messi is evident by his devotion to his team both at the club as well as at the national level. Although he has faced challenges and changes in the team's dynamics Messi has always remained faithful and committed to his team who he leads by example, and never failing to deliver his best in the playing field.

What we can take away from Messi's determination is that failures and difficulties happen in every life. But it's the way you respond to challenges that determines the person we are. If we are resilient, maintaining an optimistic mindset and not giving up, we are able to overcome the odds and accomplish our objectives. Messi's life is testimony to the strength of perseverance and provides a source of inspiration not to lose faith, regardless of the difficulties we encounter.

LEADERSHIP and TEAMWORK

Another important life lesson that to learn by studying Lionel Messi is the importance of teamwork and leadership. While he's an outstanding individual athlete, Messi understands the significance of being part of in a group and is a role model for others.

In the field Messi's leadership qualities are evident by his capacity to inspire and inspire his team. He is a role model by consistently showing a good commitment to work, and unwavering determination to achieve quality. His behavior inspires others close to him to strive for the best they can and work towards achievement.

On the other side of the court, Messi shows leadership characteristics through his participation in decisionmaking for the team and the ability to bring people together and connect his teammates. Messi fosters a feeling of unity and camaraderie, creating an environment that is positive and encouraging that allows for collective achievement.

Messi's appreciation of the value of teamwork goes beyond the immediate group. He is aware of the importance of teamwork and cooperation for achieving a common goal. If it's to represent his nation or taking part in charity initiatives Messi makes use of his influence to inspire cooperation and have an impact on greater size.

The lessons we can draw from Messi's teamwork and leadership is that the success of a team isn't just dependent on the individual's talent but on the capacity to collaborate and motivate other players.

Chapter 18: Humanitarian Work It Is The Leo Messi Foundation

Lionel Messi's charitable work with Leo Messi Foundation Leo Messi Foundation is a testimony to his kindness and determination to have an impact in the world. The foundation was established in 2007 focuses on enhancing education and health accessibility for children who are vulnerable.

One of the main aspects of Leo Messi Foundation is education. Leo Messi Foundation is providing education opportunities. They believe that education can be an extremely effective method of breaking this cycle, and providing opportunities to build an improved tomorrow. They have built schools in Argentina that provide an education of the highest quality to students who might not have access to education otherwise. They also fund the development of educational initiatives and programs, which aim to help children become empowered through the process of learning.

Apart from education In addition to education, in addition to education, the Leo Messi Foundation is committed in advancing healthcare access. The foundation has helped fund medical centers as well as initiatives to provide vital medical services to children who are who are in need. Their work has helped save lives as well as improve the wellbeing of many children.

His involvement with the foundation is more than just providing his name. He is actively involved in fundraisers, charity matches and campaigns that increase awareness and help the foundation's initiatives. His commitment to making an impact on the lives of kids who have been disadvantaged is truly inspirational.

Through his work in the field of humanitarianism, Messi teaches us the necessity to use influence and resources in order to make a positive impact on people's lives. Messi demonstrates that it isn't only measured through the accomplishments in the field, but through the positive impact that we make to the world. His commitment to charity is a constant reminder that everyone has the ability to change the world, regardless of size or insignificant.

Initiatives for Education and Health Care

Lionel Messi has been involved in a variety of initiatives that promote accessibility to healthcare and education specifically by the Leo Messi Foundation. These are a few instances:

1. Construction schools Leo Messi Foundation: The Leo Messi Foundation has constructed schools in Argentina which provide students with a quality education. The schools are designed to provide an environment of learning that is nurturing for children with limited resources who might never have the chance otherwise.

2. Educational and Scholarship Programs Messi's foundation provides scholarship opportunities and also supports programs

that aim to empower kids to be successful in their learning. They offer financial aid to students with a poor background and help them pursue their studies and realize their full potential.

3. Medical centers and healthcare support Apart from education in addition to healthcare support, the Leo Messi Foundation has funded hospitals and programs to increase access to healthcare for the most vulnerable children. They fund projects to provide the most essential health services, such as surgical procedures, medical treatment and treatments.

4. Awareness Campaigns Messi actively takes part in awarenessraising campaigns that highlight how important education as well as health care. With his powerful platform, he raises the awareness of difficulties faced by children who are not privileged and inspires other people to contribute to those causes.

In promoting these programs, Messi demonstrates his commitment to improve the lives of kids by offering them essential educational opportunities as well as better accessibility to health care. His actions serve as a model for other people to join in similar efforts and have a positive effect within the society.

CONTRIBUTION to NATURAL DISASTER RELIEF

Lionel Messi has also made important contribution to aid initiatives. Let us look at a few of his contributions:

1. Earthquake Relief Messi is actively active in assisting efforts to help victims of earthquakes in various regions of the globe. He, for instance, donated an enormous amount of money to restore areas damaged by the devastating earthquake that struck Nepal during the year 2015.

2. Flood Relief: In the year 2017, Messi donated a considerable amount to help those impacted by the devastating floods that hit his native country, Argentina. His donation provided essential items, shelter and

assistance to those people affected by the floods.

3. Humanitarian Aid Messi's foundation, called the Leo Messi Foundation, has participated in the provision of assistance to the victims of natural catastrophes. The foundation has supported projects that give immediate aid like water, food, and medical care to those suffering from floods, hurricanes as well as other natural disasters.

4. Campaigns for Fundraising: Messi has also participated in campaigns for fundraising to collect funds for relief from natural disasters. His influence and fame to inspire people to help and assist those affected by the disaster.

By his involvement in the relief effort for natural disasters, Messi has shown his dedication to aiding the needy and making a an impact in the times of crises.

AFFECT ON OTHER'S

ROLE MODEL AFFIRMED FOOTBALLERS

Lionel Messi has had a major impact on footballers from around the globe. Messi has been an inspiration to thousands of young athletes dreaming to reach the top levels of the game. This is the ways Messi is an example and role model for young athletes:

1. Skills and talent: Messi's incredible skills and ability on the field have captured fans of all ages. His incredible dribbling ability, precision passing and goalscoring capability have established new standards for the sport. Future football players look up to the player and attempt to replicate his methods and styles of play.

2. Ethics and commitment to the game Success of Messi is not just due to the natural talents of his players, it is also due to his remarkable commitment to work and determination. The player is renowned for his constant training regime and determination to continue improving. The younger players appreciate his commitment and realize that

hard work is an essential ingredient to getting to their personal ambitions.

3. The sportsmanship of humility and respect
In spite of his huge successes, Messi remains so humble and caring. He is usually averse to controversy and exhibits good sportsmanship at and off the field. His humility is a great instruction for football players who are aspiring, informing them that their success must be achieved with humbleness and respect to the team, their sport as well as opponents and supporters.

4. In the face of challenges: Messi's journey is not without obstacles. Since his earliest years it was his responsibility to overcome physical limits and show that he was worthy in a game that was dominated by bigger players. His story is one of determination and perseverance, which encourages younger players to confront their own difficulties by overcoming them with determination and courage.

5. Giving back and Philanthropy: Messi is involved in many charitable initiatives and has demonstrated a dedication to make a difference beyond the playing field. With his Lionel Messi Foundation, he helps fund healthcare and education initiatives that help children who are vulnerable. His life is a model for future footballers and encourages players to make use of their talents to benefit society.

The overall effect on football players who are aspiring is huge. Messi is an inspirational role model with his extraordinary capabilities, determination and humility, as well as his capacity to face challenges and a commitment to helping others. The influence of Messi extends far beyond his football achievements in inspiring youngsters to pursue excellence and to make an impact on their lives as well as the communities they live in.

Influence on young athletes

Lionel Messi has had a huge influence on youngsters across the world and has inspired generations of future footballers. Let us look at how Messi is now an inspirational source for numerous young athletes

1. Incomparable Skills: The Messi's amazing abilities on the field of football have been awestruck by young athletes all over the world. His speed, agility as well as his dribbling abilities, exact scoring, and dazzling goals show a level ability that is unparalleled. Many young players study the techniques of his master and try to emulate his play style in hopes of achieving the same level of skill.

2. Affirmation and Integrity The success of Messi is the testament to his unwavering devotion and unwavering work ethic. The soccer star is renowned for his extensive training regime and determination to continue improving. This is an excellent instruction for youngsters and demonstrates that dedication persistence, discipline and discipline are the key to achieving success.

3. Respect and humility: Despite his incredible talent and achievements, Messi remains

humble and exhibits exceptional sportsmanship in and out of the court. He treats his opponents, teammates as well as officials with respect and sets an excellent example for younger players. His humility shows young athletes to be kind and considerate is as crucial as winning.

4. The road towards success isn't free of obstacles. At a very young age the player was challenged by physical limitations as well as skeptics who doubted his abilities because of the height of his frame. However, Messi overcame these obstacles with determination and an unwavering energy. Athletes in the young age, who are facing the same obstacles and fears look for inspiration from Messi's determination to conquer the odds.

5. The global impact of Messi's work is far more than his achievements in the field. Being a worldrenowned athlete and a global celebrity, he's used his fame to draw focus to crucial issues and create a significant impact. The philanthropy he has done, with initiatives

that aim to improve medical and education for children, motivates athletes to make use of their achievements to impact the world.

In the end, Lionel Messi's impact on the next generation of athletes is huge. With his unparalleled abilities, determination and humility, as well as his resilience and dedication to making an impact in the lives of others his game, he's become an inspirational figure for young footballers across the globe. The influence of Messi extends far beyond football by influencing the mindset and goals of the young athletes as well as inspiring players to follow their goals by pursuing their goals with determination and passion.

Chapter 19: Affairs And Football Balancing

The marriage and parenthood

Lionel Messi has shown a impressive ability to combine his professional football schedule alongside his private life, that includes marriage and parenting. This is the way Messi can manage to keep a balance between soccer and his family life:

1. The wife of Messi, Antonela Roccuzzo, has provided a steady and supportive support throughout his playing career. A strong and understanding companion who is able to share the joys as well as the challenges that come with his journey in football is vital. Antonela has always been always there for Messi by providing his emotional support as well as the stability.

2. Family Time: In spite of the hectic schedule of his life, Messi prioritizes spending quality time with his family. He is aware of the necessity to balance his work and spending time with his family and wife. When it comes

to family gatherings and vacations or enjoying a relaxing time together, Messi values these moments and prioritizes them.

3. The privacy and routine Messi along with his wife lead an unassuming lifestyle, avoiding them from the glare of media attention. It helps them establish a rhythm and feel of routine, helping Messi keep a balance between work and family. He can concentrate on his professional career as well as be a part of his life with his family.

4. Flexible and adaptable A professional footballer frequently requires you to adapt to hectic schedules and traveling. Messi has mastered the complexities of football by flexing and incorporating the family of his players in the most effective way. It doesn't matter if it's taking them to soccer games or changing the timing of his training sessions in order to meet family commitments Messi seeks to achieve an environment that is beneficial to all.

5. A Support Systems: Messi is backed by a solid network of support that includes the immediate family members as well as close family members and reliable advisers. They play an important role in helping him to manage his personal and professional life. The support system ensures Messi is able to rely on his team whenever he needs them, which allows him to concentrate on his family obligations and soccer.

In the end, Lionel Messi demonstrates an ability to combine his soccer professional life with family time by relying on the help of his wife, prioritizing family time, ensuring privacy while being flexible and relieving on a robust family support system. Through this method, Messi is able to achieve his goals and also enjoy the affection and support from the people he loves.

CONTINUED RELATIONSHIPS DURING FAME

Despite the fame and popularity, Lionel Messi has managed to remain in touch with his friends by prioritizing the family values. Let's look at the way Messi has gotten his fame and success and success while maintaining his family ties:

1. Grounded Family Foundation: Messi's family members have played a crucial function in helping him stay focused throughout his entire journey. They've taught his a strong set of values as well as provided the needed support to ensure that he is rooted, even in the midst of his status as a celebrity. Family values like these are helping him to maintain the illusion of normality and maintain his friendships.

2. Maintaining an Inner Circle Close: Messi recognizes the significance of maintaining an intimate circle of friends. He has a trusted and reliable circle of advisors and friends who have been around him from the beginning of his career. They help Messi with a sense trust and security, which helps his navigate the difficulties of fame.

3. Privacy and boundaries: Messi is a firm believer in privacy and tries to keep some

level of privacy within his private life. He is aware of the importance in securing the people he loves from scrutiny by the media as well as allowing them to enjoy a an air of security with their friends. Through establishing limits, Messi can preserve the personal and genuine nature of the relationships he has.

4. Quality Time: Despite a busy work schedule Messi puts in an attempt to make time with his family and friends. He is committed to creating memorable experiences and memories for his friends and family, whether that's during vacations as well as celebrations or spending time with them. The commitment to spend time with his family strengthens the bonds between his family and friends, as well as reinforces his family's values.

5. Communication and Support: Messi maintains open lines of communication with loved people and seeks out their assistance in times of need. Messi is aware of how important it is to nurture connections with

those around him and keeping them in contact throughout busy or difficult moments. With a robust network of support and keeping communications open, Messi makes sure that his connections prosper amidst the celebrity.

As a summary, Lionel Messi has successfully preserved his friendships amidst all the attention through a focus on family values. With a solid familial foundation and keeping his circle of friends close, respecting limits and privacy, making an effort to be with his loved ones as well as fostering communication and support, Messi has been able keep meaningful relationships with the people closest to him. The efforts of Messi show his commitment to his family and friends as well as his determination to live up to his values. to him.

Legacy and future endevours

Lionel Messi has made significant contributions to the game of football. He has left an incredible legacy. These is a selection of his most notable achievements and future plans:

1. Recordbreaking achievements: Messi holds numerous records on both the team and at the individual at the individual level. He has received numerous Ballon d'Or awards, becoming the player to have the most wins ever in history. Messi has had the highest number of goals over the course of the calendar year, and has the record for the highest number of goals for one club, in addition to. This has solidified his status among the best footballers ever.

2. Innovative style of play and Style of Play: Messi has revolutionized the game by introducing his own unique way of playing. His control of the ball close to where it is and dribbling abilities that are unbeatable and his agility to quickly change direction are often aweinspiring to defenders. The way that he plays the game has inspired generations of players to follow a similar game style that emphasizes talent, innovation and style.

3. Team success: Messi has played a significant role in the development of his team, FC Barcelona, leading them to numerous international and domestic championships. His efforts have seen Barcelona achieve numerous La Liga titles, Copa del Rey awards, and UEFA Champions League titles. Messi's capacity to boost the performances of his teammates has contributed to the team's collective success.

4. Charitable Initiatives Messi is actively engaged in charitable activities, utilizing his name and fame to help make a difference. Through his foundation for charitable causes which he founded, he has contributed to a variety of initiatives, with a particular focus on health and education of the children who have been disadvantaged. Messi's charitable endeavors demonstrate his dedication to helping others and making a positive impact on people's lives.

5. Future Ambassadorial Position: After an illustrious career in football, Messi has the

potential to play the role of an ambassador within football. He has the potential to become a powerful persona, using his expertise as well as his knowledge and platform to encourage and coach younger players. His leadership abilities and enthusiasm for soccer will make him a perfect fit for job, and the player can contribute to the growth and development of the game.

To conclude, Lionel Messi has made important contributions to the game of football with his recordbreaking feats, a unique approach to playing, team performance as well as charitable efforts, which has his potential to play ambassadorial positions. His reputation in the role of one of football's most renowned players of all time is now secured and he is able to leave a lasting influence on the game by his next endeavors.

PLANS THAT GO ABOVE PLAYING CAREER

His lasting impact on football transcends his playing days because he has already made himself an important figure in the field of football. These are a few of the things that demonstrate Messi's lasting influence and the plans he has for his future beyond his professional career

1. Commercial and brand ventures: Messi has leveraged his international recognition to create his own image. He has formed partnerships with many companies and sponsors, showing his influence outside the game. Messi's popularity has enabled the team to consider business opportunities, like his own clothing line as well as collaborations with famous firms. The business ventures he has launched are set to flourish even after his retirement.

2. Development and Football Academy: Messi has expressed a determination to aid in the development of promising young players through the creation of football academies. They aim to provide highquality coaching and mentoring to footballers who want to become professional, developing their abilities and encouraging the development of their talents.

The initiative is a reflection of Messi's dedication to give his time to football and leaving behind a legacy of developing talent.

3. Philanthropic Achievements: Messi has made significant donations to the philanthropic sector throughout his career specifically through his foundation for charitable causes. In addition to his football career the soccer star is likely to extend his efforts in philanthropy. The foundation of Messi focuses on solving problems of social justice and improving the life of children who are at risk. His influence on the world will never cease to have a positive effect on the lives of those least fortunate.

4. The role of Football Administration: Given Messi's extensive knowledge of the game and the experience he has gained playing at the highest level could he consider taking the role of the administration of football. Be it as a coach, advisor, or even an ambassador for the game, Messi has the potential contribute to the advancement and management of the

game. His reputation as an influential player within the soccer community will influence the direction of the game.

5. Awakening the Future Generations The success of Messi and his unmatched skills have been a source of inspiration for countless football players around the globe. In addition to his professional profession, his lasting influence continues to motivate and inspire young athletes to chase their goals and aim for perfection. The impact of Messi as a rolemodel will be felt by generations to follow.

The the lasting influence of Lionel Messi extends beyond the field of play. Through his commercial and brand initiatives, football academy as well as philanthropic ventures, the possibility of a role in the football administration as well as his inspiring personality, Messi will create a lasting impression within the field of football. His goals beyond football show his dedication to creating positive changes and to determine the direction of the game.

Chapter 20: Club Career

Barcelona

2003-2005: Make it to be a member of the first team

"It appeared like he'd played with us for all his existence."

Barcelona's assistant coach Henk Ten Cate during Messi's debut for the first team.

The main focus of this story is one of the most amazing players in football, Lionel Messi, whose journey to greater heights began in the amazing 2003-04 season for Barcelona.

When he was just sixteen, Messi began a rapid rise through the ranks at the club he loved. He wowed the fans with his talents, and not only on the one but in four youth teams. He showcased his talents with one awe-inspiring season. It was impossible not to pay attention when he was awarded the honor"the tournament's "player of the competition" during four preseason international tournaments, during his time with Juveniles B.

In the next few days, the world of football was buzzing with excitement as Messi's spellbinding magic took place in the pitch. The club promoted him to the prestigious Juveniles A squad, where the player continued to amaze all those who saw his talent. After just 11 league matches He scored 18 goals. This set the foundation for a rapid ascend to fame.

But, fate promised a greater reward for the young ace. While on international duty it was fate's turn to intervene, and the team that was drained was looking for reinforcements from their promising young players. Lionel Messi was among the promising young players selected to fill the void and he brought his amazing talents onto the stage of professional soccer.

The pivotal moment occurred in a crucial training session. The setting was created as Messi was just a young Messi was matched against the seasoned players from the team. French player Ludovic Giuly was a part of the action and was amazed by the talent of the young magician. Although he had to endure a series of brutal attacks, Messi stood tall and determined, never letting up and displaying incredible resilience. He swung past players like they were puppets hanging from strings, and left the crowd awestruck. The team's best center-backs shivered at the top of their lungs in anticipation of the extraordinary talent. The player appeared to have came from a different planet and was a celestial creature who adorned the earth by bringing his divine talent.

The day was awe-inspiring, the young Messi played his first game in the team's first squad during an informal match against Jose Mourinho's Porto. At the end of the 75th minute Messi walked onto the prestigious field, and from the moment he touched his ball it became clear that something special was happening right in front of the crowds at their feet. He crafted opportunities with stunning accuracy and was close to scoring a stunning goal.

The stunning performance of Messi has left the technical team in awe The technical staff was captivated, and he received the unique privilege of working each day in Barcelona B, which is the team's reserve in addition to regular sessions with the legendary first team. A veteran player named Ronaldinho, shrewdly recognized Messi's extraordinary talent and in a fervent manner, stated that Messi's young talent could surpass his own greatness. The words of a footballing legend only ignited the flame inside Messi as he set off in a quest of self-discovery and development.

In the midst of fate's intricate web, Messi found an unexpected friend in Ronaldinho whom he affectionately called Messi "little brothers." This bond of friendship eased Messi's way into the top first-team, and allowed Messi to thrive and flourish within the world of giants.

The story of Lionel Messi's climb to fame began a story of victories, struggles and the constant search for excellence. In his quest to improve and push the boundaries of human abilities, no one did people realize that we were witnessing the creation of a legend that could change the course of soccer's history.

Each step he made his fans watched with awe, amazed by the majesty of his skill. As Messi moved across the opposition's defenses and left the footprints of his fallen adversaries that he left behind and capturing the soccer fans across throughout the world were captured by the hypnotic beauty of this unimaginable skill.

Messi performing against Malaga in 2005.

To reach his goals to reach his goal, He was a part of Barcelona C, along with Juveniles A, hoping to get more game experience. The adventure began with a memorable game on the 29th of November when Messi played his first match with the third team. Messi did everything he could to help to get them out of the downswing zone within the Tercera Division. In this period Messi showed his extraordinary ability, scoring five goals in only 10 games. The highlight in his professional career came with an incredible three-goal haul in an exciting Copa del Rey match, in spite of being closely supervised by the legendary Sergio Ramos of Sevilla. It was becoming apparent that the world would be aware of the young soccer star.

As his development was apparent, Messi was awarded his debut professional contract on the 4th February 2004, and it will run through 2012. The contract also included the buyout clause EUR30 million. This was a testimony to his talent and potential. Like the stars had at a crossroads, destiny has more to offer his future. A month later, on the 6th March, he was offered with a chance to be a part of Barcelona B, in Segunda Division B, and consequently the buyout clause was raised up to EUR80 million. While he only played 5 matches with the B team during the season, he couldn't get the ball. But the knowledge gained was valuable, which fueled his drive to improve.

In the era of his time, Messi had a disadvantage in physical strength in comparison to his rivals. He was often bigger and more imposing, making difficult for him to stand his ground in the court. Instead of becoming discouraged, he transformed his frustration into an opportunity to build muscular strength and endurance. Every day, he pushed on with his training and never gave his goal. His determination and strength are unsurpassed.

The season was drawing towards a close Messi was recalled to the junior teams. Here he played a key role in leading Juveniles B to victory, taking home the league crown. The talent of the player was evident, and at the close of the season, he recorded an astounding 36 goals in the official competitions of all five of his teams. All of the world was now witnessing the extent of his capabilities.

In the following season of 2004-2005, the Messi's place as a player in his place in the Barcelona B squad was secured as he appeared in 17 games and scored six times throughout the year. But, the break that he was hoping for with the first squad had not been granted until this point. However, the senior players were convinced of his talent and urged the manager, Frank Rijkaard, to promote the promising young player. After taking the advice of their players into account Rijkaard took a risky decision to transfer Messi from his regular place to the left wing however, the player was hesitant regarding his decision.

The tactical shift opened numerous possibilities for Messi. He was able to slice into the inside of his left foot, to launch devastating shots. It was quite an achievement as well as Messi quickly proved his merits. On the 16th of October, only 17 years, 3 months, and two days old, he played his debut in the league against Espanyol making him the smallest footballer to ever represent Barcelona in an official match. In his role as a substitute, he took advantage of every moment he spent in the field, surprising all with his abilities.

Through the entire year, he appeared in nine times for the initial team. He played an average that was 244 minutes. The highlight of his season was an unforgettable UEFA Champions League debut against Shakhtar Donetsk. The highlight of the season came at the beginning of May 1st, 2005 when he scored his very first official goal in the game against Albacete due to the assistance of legendary Ronaldinho. In that moment He became the youngest scoring player for Barcelona and was a achievement that cemented his name into the history of football.

That same season, Barcelona, under Rijkaard's direction, won the title and won the title in the span of six seasons. Fans were thrilled as Messi's popularity was growing rapidly. Everyone was aware that this promising young player could have a bright future ahead of his.

So, my dear fans, this is only the beginning of an enthralling adventure that is Lionel Messi. His tale is one of endurance with talent, determination, and passion. From humble beginnings, to his rise as one of the most successful players of all time each step of his journey is awash with joy and amazement. When we dive deeper into his story, we'll be witness to more instances of joy as well as his incredible power to football's beautiful game. Be sure to check back to the next chapter in this incredible story of football!

2005-2008: Becoming a starter eleven-player

"In my whole life I've never witnessed any player with such a high level and character at this young age. Especially in the "heavy" shirt worn by one of the greatest clubs."

The aforementioned Fabio Capello is praised by the 18-year-old Messi after the Joan Gamper trophy August of 2005.

on June 24 on the 24th of June, in the dazzling city on the 24th of June, in the city of Barcelona in the city of Barcelona, a teen soccer star named Messi was celebrating his 18th birthday. He received a special present when the first time he signed a contract as a player of the senior level with the prestigious team. What delight and excitement were in the air! The contract binds him to the club through 2010 which is just a few years later than the previous contract, however there was a new twist to add some excitement to the excitement.

The story continued to be enchanting 2 months later on an unforgettable night on the 24th of August. The time was the Joan Gamper Trophy, a magnificent pre-season competition that has earned Barcelona's illustrious fame. Destiny was smiling on the young Messi when he was spotted with the other players. As the world was his spectators, he performed his soccer magic at the famous ground. In front of the formidable Juventus with the attentive eyes of Fabio

Capello He performed dazzling dance moves on the field, captivating every person in the grand Camp Nou. There was cheers throughout the stadium as a roaring ovation honored the talented young player.

However, as with any good tale, there were challenges and rivalries that were waiting to be discovered. Capello fascinated by the talent of Messi, wanted to bring him to the place of Juventus. A different story unfolds as Inter Milan emerged, waving their banners of enticement. They promised an opulent amount of EUR150 million to buy out the clause. They even promised to double the amount he earned! The plot grew more complicated and hearts of Barcelona supporters were shaken by uncertainty. However, in the moment of the decision, Messi's loyalties shined as a lighthouse, because Messi chose to remain loyal to the club he loves.

It was an enjoyable time for a while, and on September 16th it was a fairy-godmother who appeared with an extension of his contract. This was the second renewal in just 3 months. The agreement now tied Messi to Barcelona up to the year 2014. The story of Lionel Messi continued, painting the soccer world with shades that were never before seen.

In this captivating tale of love, dreams and love, the Messi's career had just began. Fans waited with baited breath for the most captivating moments only a genius such as him could create. The story of his life were turned every time he played, and everyone was amazed by a legend that was in creation.

A momentous day in the history of football, on the 26th of September the decree was signed which granted Messi the highly sought-after Spanish citizenship and, as a result the keys to open the doors of glory in football. With the right to play now and play, he wore the fabled number 19 shirt and marched onto the pitch as the right winger chosen eager to leave his contribution to the game.

Each time Messi's talent grew as he was among soccer legends such as Ronaldinho as well as Samuel Eto'o creating a formidable attack trio. Everyone was amazed by Messi's young talent who displayed his talent with epic clashes. One of them was his debut Clasico battle, an epic battle against the unstoppable Real Madrid on a crisp 19th November.

It wasn't everything; the soccer gods have more to offer Messi as well as Barcelona. The thrilling victory away against Chelsea during the final 16 of the Champions League round demonstrated his relentless will to take on every opponent. In the course of these intense fights, anger grew in Messi and he was longing to have a match with rivals other than having to face Chelsea again.

In the course of the season, his star continued to grow and his score was growing. In a momentous day on November 2nd of this year Messi made his mark into history when he scored the first Champions League goal, propelling Barcelona to an impressive 5-1 win against Panathinaikos. However, destiny did not always play fair, and in a match against Chelsea on March 2, a nagging injury was threatening to end his career.

Undying and unstoppable, Messi fought to regain his confidence and secure his spot at his place in the Champions League final. But fate was not in his favor, and he watched from afar as his teammates were able to win without his participation. The heart was heavy with grief and he was unable to savor their triumph in Paris and made a mistake that which he was later to regret profoundly.

However, even during times of struggle, Messi's illumination did not dim. When Barcelona's fortunes started to decline, the talented youngster was more radiant than ever during the 2006-07 campaign. His talents captivated the cules and the loyal fans of Barcelona and also he crafted his magic on the pitch and scored 17 stunning goals across 36 exciting matches.

However, the road towards greatness was not easy, as injury continued to haunt the talented player. The metatarsal fracture was threatening to slow his progress and leave the athlete out for three months. In spite of his triumphant return the Champions League, the opposition was relentlessly pursuing him, which led to the club's withdrawal of the tournament.

However, his determination knew no boundaries. The league season advanced the player grew stronger as his goals swung like a massive river scoring 11 times during the last 13 matches. The proof of his genius was a day to remember in March when He made history in his history for the second time, becoming the first player in twelve years to record a hat-trick during a Clasico match, saving Barcelona by securing a dramatic 3-3 draw with Real Madrid.

The heavens showered the blessings of God His dedication and proficiency earned him recognition and honour. To show their appreciation that the team bestowed the player a brand new contract which demonstrates his importance and significantly increasing his salary.

The story of Messi's brilliance was born on the date during the Copa del Rey semi-final clash against Getafe. The day was 18th April and all the world was about experience something truly extraordinary.

The game progressed and Messi discovered himself standing in a spot that was remarkably similar to the spot where Maradona was in the 1986 FIFA World Cup quarter-finals. An eerie feeling of déjà was in the air when Messi gathered the ball on the right hand side, not too far away from the mid-line. With dazzling speed and stunning grace, he started the hypnotic run and swerving his way across the field like a professional musician, playing the notes of an orchestra.

As a gazelle dancing, Messi glided past five defenses with each strike of genius, until he was confronted with fate. In a tense moment and his body pounding, he unleashed an attack that was pure magic. He landed on the net using an unorthodox shot that left the crowd breathless. The fans erupted with joy when they saw the moment that will be remembered in the football legends and a replay of Maradona's famous "Goal of the Century."

However, the story of Messi's relationship with Maradona didn't end there. A league match played against Espanyol in a day that was memorable 9th June, Messi played Maradona's spirit again. The ball soared towards the target, Messi launched himself at his goal, steering it over the confused goalkeeper using his hands, similar to Maradona's famous "Hand of God" goal at the time of the World Cup match. There was a roar of laughter and gasps. even the stars above appeared to blink in amazement at the extraordinary skill.

While Messi's fame was rising and his team, Barcelona, faced some difficulties. However, even when Barcelona suffered, Messi soared, ascending to higher heights. His ability and skill in the game led to him being dubbed "Messiah" by the passionate Spanish media. When he was just 20 He was the center of Barcelona and was a source of inspiration and optimism for soccer fans around the world.

In 2007, Messi's outstanding accomplishments were recognized by the best of awards and praises. Journalists, who were impressed by his ability, named his third highest player to win the world-renowned Ballon d'Or award, with just Kaka along with Cristiano Ronaldo in front of him. But that's not all. International managers as well as captains of national teams voted Messi second in his FIFA World Player of the year award. He was once more in the shadow of Kaka. All over the world acknowledged his excellence, and Messi's fame grew.

However, as with all epic storylines, Messi's adventure did not come without challenges. The injuries obscure his brilliance and haunt his like a ghost that remained. The 2007-08 season was a nightmare for him even though he scored sixteen goals, his campaign was affected by a hamstring tear that he sustained on a frigid December day. Unfazed, he completed an impressive return, and with a stunning performance and skill, he became the top scorer in the Champions League by scoring six times.

But fate was conspiring against him and, during the second phase of the Champions League, he once was again a victim of an injury. Expectations from the media and fans was a heavy burden on his shoulders. However, at the same time, Messi displayed unwavering determination and dedication.

The fortunes of Barcelona may have shifted this season, they might have missed some trophies but for the fans the greatness of Messi was an illuminating beacon of faith. The story of his amazing journey unfolds and leaves us awestruck with anticipation for another moment of the magic that Messi has created on the soccer field.

2008-09: First treble

The legendary Rijkaard and the skilled Ronaldinho have left the club and left the club that needed a complete overhaul. However, they didn't know that the next star of the team is about to shine more than before.

In the midst of all the departures, the young starlet known as Messi stood ready to be the center of attention. When Ronaldinho quit, the sought-after number 10 shirt made his shoulders. It was a reminder of the huge expectation that was set for him. He signed in July and put his pen to paper for an extension of his contract. He became the highest paid player of the club, earning an annual income that was EUR7.8 million.

But there was a gloom of doubt about Messi's bright prospects. Muscle injuries that he suffered repeatedly caused him to be in pain, causing him to miss a total of eight months on field between 2006 and. This was a challenge which needed to be over in order to let him unleash his full potential.

The team, eager to care for this star of player, stepped up. They introduced cutting-edge training methods as well as carefully-crafted nutrition plans as well as a balanced lifestyle routine to safeguard their star from injury. Additionally, they hired an individual physiotherapist to be with Messi on international trips as a player for Argentina to ensure his health and endurance on the field.

When these rules were in place, Messi flourished like never before. He flew above the ground, his incredible abilities enthralling fans and opposition alike. Once a sluggish player, Messi changed into an unstoppable force on the field.

Following the season despite enduring a few earlier injuries, Messi's performances were simply stunning. His incredible performances won him the prestigious position as the second-best player for the prestigious Ballon d'Or and the FIFA World Player of the Year award. Both times, he was barely missing the awe-inspiring Cristiano Ronaldo.

In the course of time his star rose, shining football fans through his incredible skill. He effortlessly maneuvered his way through the defenses and left the defenders trailing that he left behind. The ability to score goals appeared like magic as he was the symbol of hope for Barcelona soccer fans as well as football lovers all over the world.

www.ingramcontent.com/pod-product-compliance
Lightning Source LLC
Chambersburg PA
CBHW071443080526
44587CB00014B/1977